Ethnic Worlds in Select Indian Fiction

Ethnic Worlds in Select Indian Fiction

Juri Dutta

Copyright © Tezpur University, 2014

The book is the result of a research project undertaken by Dr Juri Dutta at the Centre for Assamese Studies, Tezpur University, Assam, India.

All rights reserved. No part of this book may be reproduced or utilised in any form or by any means, electronic or mechanical, including photocopying, recording or by any information storage or retrieval system, without permission in writing from the publisher.

First published in 2014 by

SAGE Publications India Pvt Ltd
B1/I-1 Mohan Cooperative Industrial Area
Mathura Road, New Delhi 110 044, India
www.sagepub.in

SAGE Publications Inc
2455 Teller Road
Thousand Oaks, California 91320, USA

SAGE Publications Ltd
1 Oliver's Yard, 55 City Road
London EC1Y 1SP, United Kingdom

SAGE Publications Asia-Pacific Pte Ltd
3 Church Street
#10-04 Samsung Hub
Singapore 049483

Published by Vivek Mehra for SAGE Publications India Pvt Ltd, typeset in 10.5/13 pts Berkeley by RECTO Graphics, Delhi, and printed at Sai Print-o-Pack, New Delhi.

Library of Congress Cataloging-in-Publication Data

Dutta, Juri, 1976–
 Ethnic worlds in select Indian fiction / Juri Dutta.
   pages cm
 Includes bibliographical references and index.
 1. Indic fiction—History and criticism. 2. Ethnicity in literature. I. Title.
 PK5423.D88   891.4—dc23   2014   2014026962

ISBN: 978-81-321-1846-6 (HB)

The SAGE Team: Supriya Das, Dhurjjati Sarma, Anju Saxena and Dally Verghese

Ethnic Worlds in Select Indian Fiction

Juri Dutta

www.sagepublications.com
Los Angeles • London • New Delhi • Singapore • Washington DC

Copyright © Tezpur University, 2014

The book is the result of a research project undertaken by Dr Juri Dutta at the Centre for Assamese Studies, Tezpur University, Assam, India.

All rights reserved. No part of this book may be reproduced or utilised in any form or by any means, electronic or mechanical, including photocopying, recording or by any information storage or retrieval system, without permission in writing from the publisher.

First published in 2014 by

SAGE Publications India Pvt Ltd
B1/I-1 Mohan Cooperative Industrial Area
Mathura Road, New Delhi 110 044, India
www.sagepub.in

SAGE Publications Inc
2455 Teller Road
Thousand Oaks, California 91320, USA

SAGE Publications Ltd
1 Oliver's Yard, 55 City Road
London EC1Y 1SP, United Kingdom

SAGE Publications Asia-Pacific Pte Ltd
3 Church Street
#10-04 Samsung Hub
Singapore 049483

Published by Vivek Mehra for SAGE Publications India Pvt Ltd, typeset in 10.5/13 pts Berkeley by RECTO Graphics, Delhi, and printed at Sai Print-o-Pack, New Delhi.

Library of Congress Cataloging-in-Publication Data

Dutta, Juri, 1976–
 Ethnic worlds in select Indian fiction / Juri Dutta.
  pages cm
 Includes bibliographical references and index.
 1. Indic fiction—History and criticism. 2. Ethnicity in literature. I. Title.
 PK5423.D88   891.4—dc23   2014   2014026962

ISBN: 978-81-321-1846-6 (HB)

The SAGE Team: Supriya Das, Dhurjjati Sarma, Anju Saxena and Dally Verghese

To all my teachers
to whom I owe my academic life

Thank you for choosing a SAGE product! If you have any comment, observation or feedback, I would like to personally hear from you. Please write to me at contactceo@sagepub.in

—Vivek Mehra, Managing Director and CEO,
SAGE Publications India Pvt Ltd, New Delhi

Bulk Sales

SAGE India offers special discounts for purchase of books in bulk. We also make available special imprints and excerpts from our books on demand.

For orders and enquiries, write to us at

Marketing Department
SAGE Publications India Pvt Ltd
B1/I-1, Mohan Cooperative Industrial Area
Mathura Road, Post Bag 7
New Delhi 110044, India
E-mail us at marketing@sagepub.in

Get to know more about SAGE, be invited to SAGE events, get on our mailing list. Write today to marketing@sagepub.in

This book is also available as an e-book.

Contents

Foreword by Professor Amarjyoti Choudhury   ix
Acknowledgements   xi

1. Introduction   1

2. The Tradition of Assamese Ethnographic Novels   33

3. Forests, Human Rights and Development: A Cross-Cultural Study of Select Novels of Yeshe Dorjee Thongchi, Pratibha Ray and Mahasweta Devi   69

4. Folkloric Materials in Ethnic Novels (With Special Reference to Narayan, Rong Bong Terang, Lummer Dai, Yeshe Dorjee Thongchi and Sishuram Pegu)   90

5. A Feminist Reading of *Kanyar Mulya* (Lummer Dai), *Alma Kabutari* (Maitreyi Pushpa), and Select Short Stories of Mahasweta Devi   111

6. Conclusion   131

Bibliography   135
Index   147
About the Author   153

Foreword

Ethnographic fictions constitute fascinating universes of their own. In these specific universes, neutrality of ethnography often withers away. Instead we are face to face with ideological and even cosmological narratives of the author's mental make-up. So comparing the representation of ethnic worlds in this genre of fiction is akin to peeping at exciting variations of the interaction of individual mind with cultural paradigms of a society.

Dr Juri Dutta, a research associate at the Centre for Assamese Studies, Tezpur University has attempted to unveil the rich and varied representations of the ethnic world. She has specifically attempted a cross-cultural investigation into select novels of noted writers, namely, Yeshe Dorjee Thongchi, Pratibha Ray and Mahasweta Devi with reference to the motifs of forest, human rights and development. In another interesting chapter, she strives to compare the select fictions of Narayan, Rong Bong Terang, Lummer Dai, Yeshe Dorjee Thongchi and Sisuram Pegu in regard to the use of folkloristic material in their fictions. She has also drawn absorbing parallels of the feminist echoes in the writings of Lummer Dai, Maitreyi Pushpa and Mahasweta Devi.

In the Conclusion, still deeper questions are articulated. Can we, for example, attain literary and conceptual universals through these forays into aspects of tribalhood or sisterhood? Or are these studies able to capture only specific spatiotemporal truths? Dr Dutta indulges in serious discourses covering these aspects too.

These wide-ranging attempts to grapple with the body and spirit of the ethnic worlds are sure to ease our understanding of ethnicity and its future in the increasingly globalized world.

We shall eagerly look forward to more contributions from her in this exotic arena of ethnic universes in the days to come.

Professor Amarjyoti Choudhury
Pro Vice Chancellor
Tezpur University
Napaam, Assam
India

Acknowledgements

I would like to extend my sincere gratitude to all those for whom this book could see the light of day. It gives me immense pleasure to acknowledge the support offered by Professor Mihir Kanti Chaudhuri, Honourable Vice Chancellor of Tezpur University. Apart from setting up the Centre for Assamese Studies, Professor Chaudhuri, with his vision and zeal, has been a constant source of motivation for all those of us working here. This book is the result of one of the first research projects undertaken at the Centre. My sincere thanks go to Professor Amarjyoti Choudhury, Honourable Pro Vice Chancellor of Tezpur University as well as the Chairman and Coordinator of the Centre for Assamese Studies, for his regular feedback at the time when I was working on the book. I am immensely grateful to him for writing the foreword to my book. I would like to thank the members of the then Advisory Committee, Professor Alak Kr Buragohain (Present Vice Chancellor of Dibrugarh University), Professor Madan M. Sarma, Professor Sunil K. Dutta and Professor Pradip Jyoti Mahanta for their keen interest and association in all the activities of the Centre. My former colleagues at the Centre—Dr Suranjana Barua, Assistant Professor, IIIT, Guwahati and Dr Arup Kumar Nath, Assistant Professor, Tezpur University—deserve special thanks for putting up with my idiosyncrasies. Dr Biren Das, Registrar, Tezpur University, has provided all the technical and academic support on behalf of the administration for which I shall always remain grateful to him. I am always grateful to my family members for their moral and material support. My children, Nunu and Mouman, have always been the guiding spirits for me to take up any work passionately. I would like to thank both of them for the strength I gather from them. My helping hand Sumitra Didi has been the most practical support I received during my study; she not only relieved me of the household chores but has also taken care of my children. I shall always remain grateful to her. Prince has always been my strongest pillar of support. Without his guidance it would not have been possible for me to get the book published.

Acknowledgements

I would like to extend my sincere gratitude to all those for whom this book could see the light of day. It gives me immense pleasure to acknowledge the support offered by Professor Mihir Kanti Chaudhuri, Honourable Vice Chancellor of Tezpur University. Apart from setting up the Centre for Assamese Studies, Professor Chaudhuri, with his vision and zeal, has been a constant source of motivation for all those of us working here. This book is the result of one of the first research projects undertaken at the Centre. My sincere thanks go to Professor Amarjyoti Choudhury, Honourable Pro Vice Chancellor of Tezpur University as well as the Chairman and Coordinator of the Centre for Assamese Studies, for his regular feedback at the time when I was working on the book. I am immensely grateful to him for writing the foreword to my book. I would like to thank the members of the then Advisory Committee, Professor Alak Kr Buragohain (Present Vice Chancellor of Dibrugarh University), Professor Madan M. Sarma, Professor Sunil K. Dutta and Professor Pradip Jyoti Mahanta for their keen interest and association in all the activities of the Centre. My former colleagues at the Centre—Dr Suranjana Barua, Assistant Professor, IIIT, Guwahati and Dr Arup Kumar Nath, Assistant Professor, Tezpur University—deserve special thanks for putting up with my idiosyncrasies. Dr Biren Das, Registrar, Tezpur University, has provided all the technical and academic support on behalf of the administration for which I shall always remain grateful to him. I am always grateful to my family members for their moral and material support. My children, Nunu and Mouman, have always been the guiding spirits for me to take up any work passionately. I would like to thank both of them for the strength I gather from them. My helping hand Sumitra Didi has been the most practical support I received during my study; she not only relieved me of the household chores but has also taken care of my children. I shall always remain grateful to her. Prince has always been my strongest pillar of support. Without his guidance it would not have been possible for me to get the book published.

1
Introduction

Tribe, as a group, defies an easy definition in the Indian context. When one takes into account the cultural, historical, religious and linguistic varieties that constitute the official category of 'tribe' in India, we get so diverse a picture that it is impossible to speak of tribe as a common category of humanity even within the north eastern region of India. No single term is probably enough to describe, or even refer, to the tribes of India. Even if one were to accept a term for the purpose, its normative frame may run up against numerous contradictions with the strikingly divergent history of every community living in India.

However, while much has been said about the heterogeneity of Indian tribes, not many attempts have been made to understand the circumstances and commonalities that bind them together. Though there is a lot being written by and about the tribes of India, not much attention has been given to understand the impact on these ethnic worlds of issues of indigeneity, issues of gender and also of the impact on these societies of nation-building and development exercises that have been undertaken in different parts of the country in the post-Independence phase and the ways in which all of these have been represented in the regional literatures of this vast country. Unfortunately, a large chunk of these immensely significant literary works is yet to be translated into English to facilitate its accessibility to readers outside the region.

Literary texts are representations of life and they come into being through the convergence of historical and cultural contexts and world-views. Having said this, I do not, of course, believe that a literary text is to be uncritically assumed as an 'authentic' representation of life. But it is a fact that literary texts do give direct or indirect expression to the worldviews of cultures. A comparative study of literature that takes into account the historical, cultural, and aesthetic contexts enables a clearer understanding of other cultures. Many novels have been written on the life and society of the tribes in North East India. Assamese novels, representing the lives of different tribes of the region, have fetched various regional and national awards. The customs, traditions, rites and rituals of the tribes find expression in different novels of India written by writers, some of whom actually belong to the communities about which they write. I have discussed a few select novels of India that represent the ethnic life of different communities of the country. For the purpose of this book, I have taken for discussion a few Assamese novels along with a few select non-Assamese novels based on the lives and societies of tribes and attempted a comparative study by contextualizing each of these pieces of fictions against the socio-cultural and historical background of the times. While analyzing the novels, my primary focus will be on the issues of ethnicity, gender and nationalism in the fiction depicting the ethnic worlds of various communities.

Before discussing the representation of ethnicity in Indian novels, it is imperative to address the problem concerning the idea of tribe and its relationship with ethnic identity in the Indian context. My reading is informed by recent theoretical understanding of the idea of representation whereby it will be seen as a political project and not, as was traditionally believed, to be a simplistic process of transference of knowledge and information. Who represents whom and to what purpose are political questions that are related to the intimate relationship between knowledge and power. Representation and appropriation of voice is a difficult task for all writers. Sneja Gunew (1994: 31) points out that we use the term 'representation' in at least two senses: as the depiction of a subject and as delegation (when someone speaks for a group or individual). Writers and critics who are delegates for marginal or minority groups may find themselves in the situation of Gavino Ledda—from their position of power in the hegemony of Western civilization, how can they really speak for a powerless group? In using the language of the dominant culture and the discourse of sophisticated theory, can they still address the concerns of the marginal community? With every university degree there is an ever-widening gap between the writer and his/her community. And so we can see that the only concrete links this person may have with these original roots is to try to speak with and for these people. The task is not unproblematic (Paci, 1985: 47).

What follows is a brief survey of some of the major concepts that have been used in the book. It would be prudent to start off by discussing some of the core ideas that inform my position as a researcher. The concepts of tribe and ethnicity in the Indian context need to be understood and analysed.

Tribe

The Chambers 21st Century Dictionary (1997: 1504) defines the word 'tribe' as "a group of people, families, clans or communities who share social, economic, political, etc. ties and often a common ancestor and who usually have a common culture, dialect and leader". According to *The New Millennium Pronouncing Anglo-Assamese Dictionary* (2002: 843), 'tribe' is a large family that has descended from a common ancestor. Tribe is here defined as a primitive race or group of related families governed by a chief. Anthropologists have, however, defined 'tribe' differently. Obviously, therefore, the concept of tribe cannot be homogenously defined even within the country, not to talk of the world, as there is dissimilarity of opinion amongst scholars.

Majumdar and Madan (1988) defines tribe as a group with territorial affiliation, practising endogamy, with no specialization of functions, united in language or dialect, recognizing social distance with other tribes, or castes, and above all, conscious of a homogeneity of ethnic and territorial integration. In his article 'Transformation of Tribes and Analogous Social Formations' (1992: 28), B.K. Roy Burman says:

> The term (tribe) refers to a stage of social formation in an evolutionary scheme of development of technology, knowledge of and capacity for control of the forces of nature, method of transmission of the same, perception of man's relation with man and with nature and scale of organization of social groups.

It has been already said that anthropologists, historians, political theorists, sociologists, and others are yet to arrive at a clear and general definition of tribe having wide acceptance. The disagreement is stronger today than it was in the past due to their study of greater variety of societies at present. In *Society and Politics in India: Essays in a Comparative Perspective* (1999), Andre Beteille says that in the study of Indian tribes, the anthropologists do not confine themselves to the present or even to the recent past, but go back to medieval times.

Morton Fried (quoted in Beteille, 1999: 62) argues that the definition and concept of tribe used by the anthropologists are inherently ambiguous. Lewis Henry Morgan's definition of tribe which Godelier repeats is that a tribe is a totally organized society (quoted in Beteille, 1999: 61). When we speak of a tribe as a completely organized society, we assume that there are boundaries separating the tribes from each other. However, it is not clear what the nature of these boundaries is as there is no such clear boundary between one tribe and another as that between a tribe and a non-tribe.

Fried also puts forward his argument against the opinion that each tribe has its own distinctive language which defines its boundaries (quoted in Beteille, 1999: 64). There are well-known examples of people speaking in the same language, being divided into several endogamous groups as well as examples of people intermarrying though their native languages are different. Moreover, some of the tribes have no separate language of their own but use the language prevalent in the region they inhabit, particularly in the states of Rajasthan and Gujarat.

Fried's argument, therefore, represents neither a definite type of society nor a definite stage of evolution. He defines tribe as a kind of secondary phenomenon:

> ...[M]ost tribes seem to be secondary phenomenon in a very specific sense: they may well be product of processes stimulated by the appearance of relatively highly organized societies amidst other societies which are organized much more simply. (quoted in Beteille, 1999: 65)

In the opinion of Andre Beteille, in a country like India where tribe and civilization coexist, being a tribe has been more a matter of remaining 'outside' state and civilization whether by choice or necessity, than of attaining a definite stage in the evolutionary advance from the simple to the complex (quoted in Xaxa, 2003: 376).

The study of groups that later came to be described as 'tribes' began with the establishment of the Asiatic Society of Bengal in 1874. Vidyarthy divides the phase of research on tribes in India into three phases (quoted in Xaxa, 2003: 373). The period from 1874 to 1919 is considered by him as the formative period. He identifies the latter two phases as the constructive (1920–1949) and analytical phases (1950 onwards). In the post-Independence period, there was a deluge of literature emanating from three main sources—the Anthropological Survey of India, university departments of Sociology and Anthropology, and the tribal research institutes that were set up in states having a substantial population of tribes.

In the opinion of some anthropologists, the categories of caste and tribe are just 'colonial constructions' in the sense that the character of these groups was solidified by the British through the process of classification and enumeration (Xaxa, 2003: 374). There were different social groups corresponding to those identified as tribes in pre-colonial period too. But such groups which had distinct local and regional nomenclatures (for example Santhals or Nagas) were not categorized together under the general category of 'tribe'. In this sense, the category of 'tribe' is part of the modern consciousness brought into being by the colonial state and confirmed by its successor after Independence.

When the British began writing on the Indian society, the term 'tribe' was used in two senses. First, it was used to refer to a group of people claiming descent from a common ancestor. Second, it was used to refer to people or communities living in 'primitive' or 'barbarous' conditions. In the 18th century, the terms 'tribe' and 'caste' were used synonymously. In the census undertaken in 1891, the favoured term was 'forest tribe' (quoted in Xaxa, 2003: 375). In the succeeding censuses, attempts were made to formalize the distinction between 'tribe' and 'caste' but the difference remained ambiguous and inadequate.

In any case, though the terms 'tribe' and 'caste' were used synonymously, the British treated the tribes as 'different' from the rest of the Indian population. For the convenience of the colonial administration, separate laws were framed for those groups who were treated as tribes. Jaganath Pathy, in his article 'Tribal and Indigenous Peoples of the World' (1992: 13), rightly says "...who is a tribal depends much on the administrative definitions adopted by different governments".

In contrast, anthropologists have viewed the concept of 'tribe' differently—as a whole society with certain features, even though the idea of evolutionary progress of all human societies did find favour with many of them. From the point of view of some anthropologists, such as Honigmann, the society of a tribe seems to be more or less homogenous with common government, language, culture, customs, etc. (quoted in Xaxa, 2003: 375). For some others, like Sahlins, a tribe is distinguished by the absence of state-like features in its social organization, marked instead by segmental features (quoted in Xaxa, 2003: 375). Godelier views a tribe as a stage in the evolution of society, while for Fried, tribe is only a kind of secondary phenomenon acquiring its form and identity from some external source (quoted in Xaxa, 2003: 375). In the Indian context, the classification between a tribe and a non-tribe is administrative rather than anthropological. Hence, tribes are treated as those groups that are enlisted in the Indian Constitution in the list of Scheduled Tribes (Dutta, 2012: 12). The present list shows 461 tribes, out of which 174 have been identified as subgroups. The 1991 census estimated their population at 67,758,000 constituting 8.01 per cent of the total population (Xaxa, 2003: 379).

Taking into account all the preceding views of anthropologists and sociologists regarding the word 'tribe', we fail to arrive at a broad definition. We may come close to agreeing with B. Saraswati's definition of tribe as referring to a

> ...constellation of somewhat reformed aspects of primitive life, generally constituting a homogenous unit, speaking a common language, claiming a common ancestry, living in a particular geographical area, lacking in scientific knowledge and modern technology, and having a social structure based on kinship. (1991: 13)

The definition specifies that tribe, in relation to 'modern' society, is "a separate humanity" (Saraswati, 1991: 13). However, we may have reservation about accepting the definition, particularly in relation to the idea of the lack 'in scientific knowledge and modern technology'. All said and done, "Finding a definition of 'tribe' that will fit all the existing communities that have been described as tribes has proved to be difficult.... Even the best ethnographers habitually confused tribe with caste, which, on any reasonable assumption, is a different kind of social category" (Beteille, 1998: 187).

From 'Tribe' to 'Ethnic Group'

The idea of tribe as a 'separate humanity' has slowly given way to 'ethnicity' which is a more recent term, generally used to refer to kinship, group solidarity and common culture. Tribes are units of organization that are based internally. Ethnicity, on the other hand, is not just about how a people describe themselves but also how they are described by others, in relation to other cultural groupings. Thus, when it comes to issues of literary representation, the term 'ethnicity' is likely to find greater acceptability than 'tribe'. However, it would be worthwhile to remember that though the term 'ethnicity' itself is new, the ideas associated with it are relatively old. The term 'ethnicity' first appeared in the 1950s in the English language. According to Hutchinson and Smith (1996: 4), it was first recorded in the Oxford English Dictionary of the year 1953.

Today, the term 'tribe' is used in a more limited sense in the academic world than the term 'ethnic group'. J. Milton Yinger (1997) identifies characteristics of a tribe as proposed by anthropologists and sociologists starting from the time of Morgan. According to the anthropologists, a tribe is small group, usually preliterate and preindustrial, relatively isolated and endogamous (with exogamous sub-title divisions). And the members of a tribe are united mainly by kinship and culture, but in many places also by territorial boundaries (Yinger, 1997: 22). In this sense tribes are not ethnic groups. Ethnic group is a more comprehensive term. Ethnic groups are "...distinguishable culturally; they are identified, by others and by themselves, as separate; and, in the fullest sense, as individuals they join in activities and share beliefs and aspirations that express their distinctiveness" (Yinger, 1997: 25).

Eric Wolf (1994: 6) has defined an ethnic group as a social entity that arises and defines itself against other social entities also engaged in the process of development and self-definition. Thus, Wolf points to the fact that ethnic groups are constructed and that their existence is always reliant on the existence of an 'other'. It is significant that the term 'ethnicity' is described in relation to its difference from other ideas or issues. Hutchinson and Smith (1996: 22) term it as an "us and them duality". Werner Sollors (1995: 288) aptly defines that ethnic identity "is logically and historically the product of the assertion that 'A is an X because he is not a Y'—a proposition which makes it remarkably easy to identify Xness".

The concept of tribe is no longer as appealing to anthropologists today as the term 'ethnic group', though the former continues to enjoy official recognition in India. According to Niezen (2003: 3), "The terms 'ethnicity' and 'ethnic group' went through a ... vogue starting in the 1960s, working their way into a profuse literature and culminating in a more recent coinage, 'ethnonationalism'." The word 'ethnic groups' has thus come to refer to "different racial or national groups which identifies them in virtue of their shared practices, norms and systems of belief" (Edgar and Sedgwick, 2008: 114). There may be of course an inherent prejudice in characterizing a group of people as 'ethnic': when a community is characterized as 'ethnic' they are usually implicitly identified as being in the minority and as possessing a set of attitudes or traditions that are different from the ones held and adhered to by the majority of a society's members. However, ethnicity can also be understood as a synonym for 'nationhood' or 'peoplehood'. In this understanding, everyone, not just minorities, belong to an 'ethnic group'.

In contrast, "'ethnicity' denotes the self-awareness on the part of a particular group of its own cultural distinctiveness" (Edgar and Sedgwick, 2008: 114). Anthropologists have commonly used criteria such as language, political organization and territorial contiguity to distinguish between cultural groups. Among other things, ethnic groups generally share myths of common origin, and they nearly always have ideologies encouraging endogamy, which may nevertheless be of highly varying practical importance.

> The term "ethnicity" is sometimes used in a general way to refer to [a] reconstituting of collective identities, but the amount of power and the political goals, choices, and surrounding contexts of ethnic groups vary

tremendously, making it nearly impossible to build globally applicable analytical models or sometimes even to get a handle on events as they happen. (Niezen, 2003: 7)

Contrary to popular assumption, Neizen (2003: 7) points out that "Not all ethnic groups or other minorities want to secede from states, and not all are violent." However, there are important ways in which distinctions can be drawn among ethnic societies "whose leaders voice unappeased discontent and unfulfilled yearnings for self-determination and whose ambitions at some level involve a rejection of the multicultural projects proposed by states and international organizations" (Niezen, 2003: 7).

Ethnicity is a contested term in the sense that in the construction of ethnic identity, the place of history, language and culture—all these factors play an important role. Stuart Hall (1997: 162) remarks, "The term ethnicity acknowledges the place of history, language and culture in the construction of subjectivity and identity." Hutchinson and Smith (1996: 6–7) identify the following characteristics of an ethnic group:

1. a common *proper name* that marks the "essence" of the community;
2. a myth of *common ancestry*;
3. a shared *history* including memories of heroes, events, and their ritualistic commemoration;
4. one or more *elements of common culture*, which need not be specified but normally include religion, customs, and language;
5. a *link* with a *homeland*, real or imagined
6. a *sense of solidarity*

It is true that ethnic identities exist around the axes of ancestry, culture and language. But these by themselves do not give us an ethnic community. It is necessary that this shared understanding of language, ancestry and culture among other things be effectively mobilized in social transactions.

> The concept of ethnicity refers to the way in which social and cultural difference, language and ancestry combine as a dimension of social action and social organization, and form a socially reproduced system of classification. (Fenton, 1999: 62)

Fredrik Barth and Ronald Cohen noted the rise to prominence of the concept of 'ethnic group' in the 1960s and 1970s respectively. However, as in the case of 'tribe', there was no agreement among scholars about the meaning of 'ethnicity' or 'ethnic group'. According to Fredrik Barth (1969: 15), ethnicity is a set of delineated boundaries between neighbouring groups, and individuals are primarily concerned with maintaining these boundaries in order to explain one's identity, in a relative, comparative manner. Ronald Cohen (1978: 388) extends Barth's assertion by explaining that ethnicity is a fluid concept by which members distinguish "in-groups" from "out-groups", and which can be in a state of constant change depending on the context. The basis of Cohen's argument, like Eric Wolf's, is that social identity is always defined in terms of an 'other'. Thus, Barth viewed ethnic identity as an "individualistic strategy" in which individuals move from one identity to another to "advance their personal economic and political interests, or to minimize their losses" (Jones, 1997: 74). In contrast to Barth, Cohen "placed [a] greater emphasis on the ethnic group as a *collectively* organized strategy for the protection of economic and political interests" (Jones, 1997: 74). Ethnicity is thus understood to be constructed within the contexts of economic and political structures and beliefs. As a social phenomenon, it is rooted in social, political and economic structures. Fenton's view is appropriate in this context:

> Groups who are ethnically identified have differential access to political power, from the natural constituency of competing political parties, and become the bearers or the targets of ethnic and racial ideologies. (1999: 6)

In many ways, the change from 'tribe' to 'ethnic group' was necessitated by the attempt to undo historical wrongs. One could argue that the use of the concept of 'tribe' was the manifestation of a perspective of colonial anthropologists which was informed by a powerful yet unseen boundary between them (the anthropologists) and the people they studied. Further, the notion of tribe relies on the evolutionary concept of culture which has increasingly, albeit understandably, come under fire. The concept of ethnicity, a politically more useful term, helps to break this unseen but telling difference between the seekers of knowledge and the object of study. Further, everyone does belong to one or the other ethnic community. Thus, the concept of ethnicity can be said to lead to a focus on cultures as fluid instead of being frozen in time and place, and it relativizes the boundaries between 'us' and 'them', between 'moderns' and 'tribals'.

The tendency to reduce the object of study into something separable and quantifiable cannot really take into account the non-measurable and non-quantifiable aspects of the cultural life of ethnic communities living in North East India. Biswas and Suklabaidya (2008: 19) mentions, "Colonial and post-colonial nation states have simply bypassed these stateless societies from the processes of cultural and political recognition, although they have been made a part of the constitutional and institutional framework of India." The ethnic groups of the North East have been granted official recognition as scheduled tribes but this has been accompanied by a deep sense of unease about their difference with the 'mainstream' cultures.

Andre Beteille has traced the historical development of the 'idea' of tribe in the Indian context. He mentions that in the 19th century, 'tribe' meant not just a "particular *type of society*" but also a particular "*stage of evolution*" (1998: 187). Today, the term 'tribe' appears to be facing stiff competition from new trends in anthropology that has ensured that today it "points less to a type of society or a stage of evolution than to the priority of settlement: where one spoke in the past of the 'tribal population' of a country, one now speaks more and more of its 'indigenous people'" (Beteille, 1998: 188). Alongside ethnicity, the concept of 'indigeneity' has gained increasing prominence in the discourses of the humanities and social sciences. Gausset, Kenrick and Gibb (2011: 135) say that

> ...the etymology of the term 'indigenous' refers to the native or original inhabitants of a country or area. Indigenous people are commonly regarded as being the first inhabitants of a given territory, or at least to have occupied it prior to successive waves of settlers.

Niezen (2003: 3) says, "The term 'indigenous' ... is not only a legal category and an analytical concept but also an expression of identity, a badge worn with pride, revealing something significant and personal about its wearer's collective attachments." Niezen (2003: 5) further points out David Maybury-Lewis's outline of the continuum ranging from "indigenous/tribal peoples to indigenous (but not tribal) peoples, to peoples stigmatized as tribal, to people considered ethnic minorities, to people considered ethnic nationalities, though they coexist in a single state". Maybury-Lewis concludes that "there are no distinctions that enable us to place societies unambiguously within these categories" (Niezen, 2003: 5). The widely circulating discourse of indigeneity revolves around the axes of the global and the local. On the global side of the discourse are such international actors as the United Nations. On the other hand, the local side of the discourse of indigeneity finds expression in the rhetoric of those who claim to be the 'marginalized' sections in the state-sponsored projects of development and forced rehabilitation.

Friedman (1999: 398) says that when one considers the global perspective "there is not much disagreement today concerning the fact that the world is pervaded by a plethora of indigenous, immigrant, sexual and other cultural political strategies aimed at a kind of cultural liberation from the perceived homogenizing force of the state." Thus Niezen (2003: 5) points out, "Indigenous peoples, like some ethnic groups, derive much of their identity from histories of state-sponsored genocide, forced settlement, relocation, political marginalization, and various formal attempts at cultural destruction." Indigeneity is thus more a matter of how one locates oneself in the world than about how one is looked at. The discourse of indigeneity "like any other discourse, enables certain articulations and, at the same time, excludes or suppresses others" (Karlsson, 2003: 406).

It can be argued that the identity of indigenous ethnic groups (that are the focus of interest in this book) are not based on universal cultural characteristics possessed by a specific group (as evidences in North East India would suggest) but are formed through discursive practices. Thus, "ethnicity is formed by the way we speak about group identities and identify with the signs and symbols that constitute ethnicity" (Barker, 2004: 63).

Literature may be seen as one of the 'signs and symbols' that constitutes ethnicity. Thus, those literary texts that overtly connect to an ethnic world can be viewed as a discursive formation on ethnicity. Ethnicity is one of the most interesting aspects of modern literature around the world and opens many new possibilities for examining texts on a comparative basis. Further, if ethnicity is a discursive formation as Barker says, it can be best analysed by looking at the literary representations of ethnicity both by 'insiders' as well as 'outsiders'.

In the course of my book, I will be mainly using the term 'ethnic group' to refer to those who people the pages of the works of fiction that I discuss. However, the terms 'tribal' and 'indigenous' are also used depending on the context. My use of 'ethnic' and 'ethnicity' is limited to the indigenous tribal people; thus, in this book, 'ethnic' refers not to any ethnic group but to those tribes that claim indigeneity. We will do well to remember though that while in most of India, the term 'tribal' is controversial, it may have wider acceptability in some parts of the country, where tribes predominate (Beteille, 1991: 57–58).

Representation

'Representation' is a term which has occupied an influential place in the understanding of literature right from the days of Plato and Aristotle. In common usage, the term is used to define literature as 'representation of life'. But in literary theory, the term 'representation' is generally used to refer to something that looks like or resembles; representation might also be used to refer to the sense of standing in place of something or someone. Representation might also be used in the sense of something being re-presented. In my present study, I look at the term from the third perspective. When I say 'representation of ethnic world', I mean the presentation of this world for a second time. The world is already there, and I am trying to see how it is 'represented' in the work of literature.

Both for Plato and Aristotle, literature is just a form of representation. There are many senses in which Plato used the word 'imitation'. Richard McKeon (1936: 5) has identified one of the more limited sense in which the term was used by Plato:

> In one of its narrowest senses Plato used the word "imitation" to distinguish poetic styles into three kinds: pure narrative, in which the poet speaks in

his own person without imitation, as in the dithyramb; narrative by means of imitation, in which the poet speaks in the person of his characters, as in comedy and tragedy; and mixed narrative, in which the poet speaks now in his own person and now by means of imitation.

For Plato, the concept of representation is much more complex. Plato too accepts that literature is a representation of life, but he believes that representations create worlds of illusion leading one away from the real things. Plato discarded poetic imitation because it is intrinsically lacking in any correspondence to real life:

> One cannot be ignorant of medicine and still be a splendid doctor ... one can be a poet without being knowledgeable ... it is not part of poets' imitative job to learn the facts about the things they write about. Since poetic imitation can be accomplished without appeal to the facts of the matter, it cannot be an imitation of a thing's true nature. (Pappas, 1995: 177)

For Plato, poetry (literature) is far removed from reality as it represents something which is already removed from reality. He argues that a poet imitates something which is already an imitation. In fact, the poet creates his art by looking at the material world around him which is already an imitation. A charge that Plato brings against poetry is that they are forms of imitation, "at a third remove from the truth" and that "these works cripple our thought and corrupt our souls" (Moss, 2007: 415). It is in this sense that for Plato, the creative artist is removed from reality. Plato believed that representation needs to be controlled or monitored. Otherwise, poetry might nurture emotions and also encourage the evil-minded:

> Plato decried the contagious effects of poets on spectators and denounced poetic imitation as "an ordinary thing having intercourse with what is ordinary, producing ordinary offspring". (Gruber, 1987: 201)

Thus, Plato levels a number of charges against poetic imitators such as the fact that they represent images far removed from the truth about what they represent. He even believes that imitation is the most dangerous of poetic charms because "it can seduce even those who generally know better" (Moss, 2007: 415).

For Aristotle, on the other hand, representation is natural to human beings, referring to all kinds of verbal, visual or musical representation. He believes that the ability to create and manipulate signs makes humans different from other animals. Aristotle's version of representation, unlike Plato's, is not a form of signification in which one posits a relation of "copy" to "original" (Halliwell, 1990: 489). The creative artist produces "likenesses". The artefact that he creates "can be perceived and understood as possessing in a fictive form, and in that sense signifying, properties of the same kinds as belong to things in the world" (Halliwell, 1990: 492).

Importantly for Aristotle, all images are mimetic in the sense of being representational. However, the 'real' and the text of representation do not bear a relationship of copy to original as we have seen. A piece of fiction is mimetic not because it aims to reflect a particular kind of society or worldview but "only insofar as it works these into a dramatized pattern of action which exhibits 'universals'" (Halliwell, 1990: 493). Thus, the Aristotelian concept of 'mimesis' or representation is of particular interest in Comparative Literature. Aristotle disagrees with Plato's view that artistic representation is a reflection of the world; in contrast, for Aristotle, appreciation of a mimetic work is about the "the way in which it presents a possible or supposed reality" (Halliwell, 1990: 493). While for Plato creative writers tend to obfuscate the difference between 'real' reality and literary reality, for Aristotle this difference is fundamentally irreconcilable.

The Marxist critic Georg Lukács, in line with Aristotle, rejects the idea of 'photographic' representation. Lukacs redefined the idea of realistic representation:

> Reality is not a mere flux, a mechanical collision of fragments, but possesses an 'order', which the novelist renders in an 'intensive' form. The writer does not impose an abstract order upon the world, but rather presents the reader with an image of the richness and complexity of life from which emerges a sense of the order within the complexity and subtlety of lived experience.
> (Selden, Widdowson and Brooker, 2005: 87)

In any case, reality cannot be comprehended without representation; through discourses, images or texts, one can perceive reality in however slippery or elusive a form. But it is also true that reality is a much more complex issue than any system of representation can possibly comprehend. If language is the means of literary representation, philosophers have argued that language too fails to represent what is real. Dale Spender, in her *Man Made Language* (1980), suggests that women have been fundamentally oppressed by a male-dominated language. There is already an acceptance of the fact that language is a treacherous medium. Thus there arises the need for creating ever new modes of representation. As a result, new theories and concepts of representation have been formulated. It can be argued that Derrida and the other poststructuralists have come to accept the Aristotelian claim that there will always be a gap, a difference between literary reality and 'real' reality. The poststructuralists, in fact, claim that it would be foolhardy to assume that there is an unchanging, unified reality that is waiting to be represented. In fact, they are more in favour of the kind of texts that accept the gap and difference between 'real' reality and literary reality than texts "that try to hide their impotence such as philosophical texts or realistic novels that claim to offer a true representation of the world" (Bertens, 2008: 107). The poststructuralists are interested in literary texts only to the extent that they can show

> ...how their seemingly realistic surface is an effect of suppression and of the suggestion they create that their readers are unified (whole) and in control of the text they are reading—either through the superior knowledge that the text allows us to have or through the ironic position that we are supposed to take up. (Bertens, 2008: 107)

The poststructuralists have textualized history. Even the past can never be available to us directly, but always in the form of "representations" (Selden, Widdowson and Brooker, 2005: 181).

In the second half of the twentieth century, structuralists, poststructuralists, postcolonialists and feminists have all contributed significantly to our understanding of what constitutes representation. Stuart Hall in his book *Representation: Cultural Representations and Signifying Practices* (1997: 15) says: "Representation is a part of the process by which meaning is produced and exchanged between members of a

culture." This process involves the use of language, of signs and images which stand for or represent things. For Stuart Hall (1997: 17),

> Representation is the production of the meaning of the concepts in our minds through language. It is the link between concepts and language which enables us to refer to either the 'real' world of objects, people or events, or indeed to imaginary worlds of fictional objects, people and events.

For him, representation is a medium or channel through which meaning production happens. He assumes that no objects or people have any stable, fixed or true meanings. Instead, the meanings are produced by human beings. And, these human beings are participants in a definite culture and therefore, have the power to make things mean or signify something.

There are a number of theories about representation or about how language is used to represent the world. Stuart Hall distinguishes between three approaches to representation. He argues that in the reflective approach, meaning is thought to lie in the object, person, idea or event in the real world, and language functions like a mirror, to reflect the true meaning as it already exists in the world (Hall, 1997: 24). According to the intentional approach, it is the author who imposes his or her unique meaning on the world through language. Words mean what the author intends they should mean. Constructional approach acknowledges that neither things in themselves nor the individual users of language can fix meaning in language. Things do not mean, we construct meaning, using representational systems-concepts and signs (Hall, 1997: 25).

In my discussion here, I will mainly use the word 'representation' both in the 'reflective' and 'constructionist' sense. However, on some occasions, my analysis might also be classified as 'intentional'. W. J. T. Mitchell remarks,

> It should be clear that representation, even purely "aesthetic" representation of fictional persons and events, can never be completely divorced from political and ideological questions.... If literature is a "representation of life," then representation is exactly the place where "life" in all its social and subjective complexity, gets into the literary work. (Lentricchia and McLaughlin, 1995: 15)

For Edward Said representation can never be exactly realistic. It can never be completely objective. Instead, they are just constructed images/ideas which need to be questioned for their ideological content. No individual or situation has a constant meaning, but their meaning is constructed both by humans depending on the context of their culture. So, meaning is created and circulated through language as a means of representation. Representation, thus, is the very process through which meanings are constructed. It can, for Said, also lead to the 'construction' of knowledge about a community or civilization. Thus, for him, Western representations of the Orient have always generated a damaging discourse which Bertens (2008: 163) defines as "a loose system of statements and claims that constitutes a field of supposed knowledge and through which that 'knowledge' is constructed".

Feminist critics have concentrated attention on how literary representations of women very often reflect gender stereotypes. We frequently come across the stereotypes of women as a seductress, or as a 'damsel in distress', or as a self-sacrificing angel, and so on. In this sense, Plato's arguments hold good even today: the way female characters are generally portrayed does not have much in common with the way women actually experience themselves. These kind of female characters clearly are *constructions* created "not necessarily by the writers who presented them themselves, but by the culture they belonged to—to serve a not-so-hidden purpose ... a perpetuation of the unequal power relations between men and women" (Bertens, 2008: 76).

I conclude this section with two quotes: one from Graham Murdock and the other from Meenakshi Gigi Durham and Douglas M. Kellner. Both the quotes substantiate and provide the basis of my argument in the book with reference to representation.

> We also need to ask who orchestrates these representations? Who is licensed to talk about other people's experience? Who is empowered to ventriloquize other people's opinions? Who is mandated to picture other people's lives? Who chooses who will be heard and who will be consigned to silence, who will be seen and who will remain invisible? Who decides which viewpoints will be taken seriously and how conflicts between positions will be resolved? Who proposes explanations and analyses and who is subject to them? (Murdock, 1999: 28)

There is no doubt that any form of literary representation is bound to raise these questions. On a slightly different note, Douglas M. Kellner and Meenakshi Gigi Durham say,

> There is no pure entertainment that does not contain representations, often extremely prejudicial, of class, gender, race, sexuality, and myriad social categories and groupings. Cultural texts are saturated with social meanings, they generate political effects, reproducing or opposing governing social institutions and relations of domination and subordination. (Durham and Kellner, 2006: xiv)

Questions of representation still involve the issues that Plato and Aristotle were trying to grapple with more than two thousand years ago. While many critics believe today that literary representation must maintain a sort of fidelity to the world of 'reality', some others argue that a literary text creates its own reality which relates to universal principles of life but is free of the burden of having to stick to surface reality. These questions are even more engrossing when one considers the fact that the present book seeks to highlight representational practices in the context of novels based on ethnic societies. Strict adherence to the 'reality' of the author's lived experience might turn a piece of fiction into an ethnographic account. However, it is also true that the 'universal' might only be evoked by reference to the 'surface realities' of life.

The Indian Novel

When we talk of the Indian novel, we generally include the wide range of fiction written by any Indian, immaterial of the language that the writer is writing in—it may be Assamese, Bengali, Malayalam, Gujarati or any other of the Indian languages. The fictions written in English by any Indian writer can also be clubbed under the category of the Indian novel. India is a multilingual country and therefore it inherited a 'multiliterary situation'. The multiliterary and multiethnic nature of Indian culture has meant that there is an absence of a singular Indian literary tradition which is expressive of a national will and representative of its heterogenous socio-cultural milieu. Instead of a definite lingual and literal tradition in India, we have a variety of literary traditions representing different regional literatures of India. On the other hand, it is also true that though the regional literatures of India in their vernacular languages pave ways for various literary traditions, national will and the ideas of nationhood very often get reflected in these writings.

In the article 'Towards a Concept of the Indian Novel: A Thematic Construct' (1989: 201), Satendra R. Singh asks, "Can there be a national literature in a multilingual situation?". We cannot arrive at a conclusion whether national literature is possible in a multilingual situation, but we can say that the ideas of nationhood is very well dealt with by the regional Indian writers in their fictions. Satendra R. Singh (1989: 208) believes that

> The novels in India, besides being a Hindi, Marathi, Tamil or Bengali novel, is also an Indian novel, dealing with an Indian situation, or is a work of an Indian writer who is himself a product of the Indian consciousness and so views events and themes from an Indian perspective.

Therefore, he suggests that we delink the text from its respective linguistic identity and unshackle the author from his 'narrow' regional literary environment.

A discussion of the novels on the ethnic worldview in the context of India should ideally begin with an account of the Indian novel in general. However, the idea of the Indian novel is as vexed and as slippery a terrain as that of the tribe. It is, first of all, very difficult to arrive at an all-inclusive definition of the Indian novel. Amiya Dev talks about such difficulties in his article 'Comparative Literature in India'. He says that India has many languages and literatures and thus represents an a priori situation and unique conditions of diversity. Dev, therefore, argues that to speak of Indian literature in the singular is problematic. He says:

> Based on history, ideology, and often on politics, scholars of literature argue either for a unity of Indian literature or for a diversity and distinctness of the literatures of India. Instead of this binary approach ... I argue

that in case of India the study of literature should involve the notion of the interliterary process and a dialectical view of literary interaction. (2000: 2)

Meenakshi Mukherjee (1984: 76) had a fitting response for those who tend to be suspicious of the intrinsic merit of the concept of the Indian novel:

> It is a critical platitude to say that the Indian novel is a derivative form, imitated from the West. This is only superficially true. A form cannot be superimposed on a culture where there is no appropriate ethos to sustain its content. The reality of the Indian social situation had to be bent to suit the exigencies of realism. The realistic novel came into existence when the tension between the individual and the society acquired a certain intensity.

However, this should not make us turn a blind eye to the universal literary concerns that Indian fiction written in various Indian languages share. Mentioning K.M. George and his edited volume of *Modern Indian Literature: An Anthology*, Shormishtha Panja (2001: 4) says that it is impossible to locate the "so-called 'Indianness' of our manifold literary expressions, although the need to discover it is frenetically underlined". In her opinion, 'Indianness' is too vague an idea "to be all convincing, particularly when George admits that this 'Indianness' is recognizable, but not easily explained or defined" (Panja, 2001: 4). While it is not easy to decide what is Indian literature or the 'Indianness of manifold literary expressions of India', it is obviously more problematic to define Indian fiction.

In a very general sense, Indian fiction includes the fiction written by Indians of any caste or community, or, in a slightly more limited sense, novels written in any official Indian language. Even novels depicting Indian lives and society, but written in English can be placed in the category of the Indian novel. However, in my study, I will exclude the category of the Indian English novel for reasons that I will not go into in detail. But for the sake of clarity, let me make the following observations. Firstly, there are not many works of fiction in Indian English Literature that depict ethnic lives. To some extent, the North East of India, with writers like Mamang Dai and Temsula Ao, is an exception. Secondly, as I will later explain, the 'Indianness' amongst many that I seek to explore lives more vibrantly in the regional literatures of India.

Unfortunately, for a large number of readers, including me, access to these novels written in various regional languages of India is provided by their English translations. I am aware that there are problems in surveying a regional literature in a colonial language such as English. Tharu and Lalitha (1993: xx), in spite of their own use of English translations, concede that the very act of representing a local culture through the medium of a more dominant one can result in reduction and homogenization.

Scholars are of different opinions regarding the concept of 'Indian Novel'; many of them campaign and vouch for the idea of the 'Indian novel' as they believe that it reflects an 'Indian consciousness'. Many others are in favour of the use of the term 'novels in India' as they believe that there cannot be a category like Indian novel as such, because in India, novels are written in many different languages, highlighting various worldviews. I have reservation regarding R. Singh's labelling of 'Indian perspective' (1989: 208) while dealing with the novels of India. I would tend to agree more with Amiya Dev (1984: 51–52) whose ideas on Indian literature can very well be applied to the concept of the Indian novel:

> It may be wrong to begin with Indian literature, for literature is language-based, to start with, though not language-contained…it may be better to call it comparative Indian literature. For Indian literature in this sense is not literature; in order to be literature it will have to be an aggregate of all literatures, which of course is absurd…Besides, as long as we cannot cook up a language called Indian, there cannot be an Indian literature as such. So Indian literature in this sense is an idea, a pedagogy, a viewing of two or more literature together.

The Indian novel (using it as an umbrella term to refer to novels written in any Indian language) came into vogue after the arrival of the British in India. The birth of the novel was in Europe and it was bound to capture the imagination of the people in the colonies. The sense of 'Indianness' was born out of the anti-colonial struggle. India, for Aijaz Ahmad (2004: 80), is a modern nation that was "the *product* of the anti-colonial movement itself and an entity that arose out of the crucible of 15 August 1947". Earlier India had always been scattered and disjointed due to the multicultural and multilingual set-up of the country. After the coming of the British, the people of the country started to feel the need of a national identity, and the concept of the nation came into being. In his article 'In Search of the Indian Novel' (1961: 607), Herbert McArthur talks of a 'spiritual wholeness' that binds India together. In the same article, McArthur mentions Nirod C. Chaudhuri and his idea of Indian identity. McArthur (1961: 608) mentions the two books *The Autobiography of an Unknown Indian* and *A Passage to England* by Nirod C. Chaudhuri and says that in these two books Chaudhuri tries to replace the "comfortable but fictitious unity with an uncomfortable but honest pluralism". We can say the same thing in case of Indian fiction too.

Some of the critics writing on the Indian novel have essentialized the notion of Indianness. Stanley Orman (1970: 61) believes that "the attitudes and values which characterize the epics, the *Mahabharata* and the *Ramayana* and classical literature are truly Indian." Quoting Hamdi Bey, he says that the Indian writer has been unable to synthesize or intelligently link himself with fully Indian values and the basics of the novel. It is pertinent for us to know what are the 'fully Indian values' and the 'basics of novel'. It is significant that neither can we identify any 'fully Indian value' which can have a wide acceptance considering the heterogeneity of regional or culture-specific values nor can we find an all acceptable definition of the 'basics of novels'.

Many scholars are in favour of establishing a concept of 'Indian' literature that is free from regional chauvinisms. In the introduction to the edited book *Handbook of Twentieth-Century Literatures of India* (1996: 8), Nalini Natarajan says,

> Comparative literature specialists within the Indian academy advance the argument for treating "Indian" literature as a unity in several ways. Uma Shankar Joshi points, for instance, to medieval India of the Bhakti period for commonalities (though in different languages) embodying "the Indian Spirit".

However, as Meenakshi Mukherjee (2008: 169) says, "A nation often gets defined by the twin processes of obliterating the differences within its boundary and by emphasizing differences with whatever lies outside the border."

The concept of 'Indian' literature as a homogenized entity might be a noble idea for the advocates of the 'unity in diversity' slogan. With regards to such a notion, I would like to propose the need to talk in terms of an ethnic literary tradition in India. In this context, it would be pertinent to quote A.K. Ramanujan:

> One way of defining diversity for India is to say what the Irishman is said to have said about trousers. When asked whether trousers were singular or plural, he said, "Singular at the top and plural at the bottom". (quoted in Guttman, 2007: 1)

Anna Guttman (2007: 1), quoting this, rightly mentions that in the context of India "what one perceives is a function of where one looks". Aijaz Ahmad (quoted in Guttman, 2007: 3) describes the Indian nation as a "process ... a terrain of struggle which condenses all social struggles, so that every organized force in society attempts to endow it with meanings and attributes".

A proper understanding of Indian fiction thus necessitates its examination against the backdrop of "the highly diverse historical trajectories [which] may simply not be available for generalizing theoretical practices and unified narratives" (Ahmad, 1994: 244). Indian literature does consist of writings that Ahmad describes as "the High textuality of the Brahmanical kind" that are traditionally considered important; but as Ahmad (1994: 244) says, it also constitutes traditions and texts that are generally excluded from the literary canon, texts and traditions that are tremendously important from a literary point of view. Such texts which are excluded from the literary canon but important from a political and aesthetic point of view will constitute the core of my discussion in this book.

Meenakshi Mukherjee highlights a problem of a different kind that faces the Indian novel today. I will conclude this section with a quotation from her book *Elusive Terrain: Culture and Literary Memory* where she says that only those Indian novels written in English or written in the indigenous languages but available in English translation would attract some attention in the outside world which are

> ...documents of culture, but only when they address issues of extreme deprivation on the basis of caste or ethnicity and gender ... in any society

at a given time there are many more issues to engage the writer but those which do not fall within the politically defined literary agenda are not likely to be export material. (2008: 187)

Thus, she believes that there is a threat that only the dramatic will gain visibility in times to come. Chakladar (2011: 3) echoes a similar view:

> It is difficult to say what the fate of literatures in the other Indian languages would have been on the global markets if there were no appreciable Indian literary output in English. It is clear, however, that contemporary Indian writers in languages other than English do not enjoy even a fraction of the international readership in translation into English that their peers from Latin America or continental Europe do.

Comparative Literature

This study will be an attempt to compare and contrast the literary voices in the margins that have challenged, or at least altered, existing literary traditions of many Indian languages. I propose to discuss the ethnic worlds in Indian fictions and to that effect, this study will take into account the fictional works on the ethnic communities of India. My study will be an attempt to look at ethnic fiction in regional literatures of India from the point of view of Comparative Literature that is informed by the writings of Steven Tötösy de Zepetnek and his concept of Comparative Cultural Studies.

The discipline of Comparative Literature has gone through a lot of troubled waters for quite often it has meant different things to different people. It has very often meant different things even to the Comparatists themselves. Way back in 1949, René Wellek and Austin Warren (1949: 38–39) had explained that

> ...comparison is a method used by all criticism and sciences, and does not, in any way, adequately describe the specific procedures of literary study ... the term "comparative" literature has covered and still covers rather distinct fields of study and groups of problems. It may mean, first, the study of oral literature, especially of folk-tale themes and their migration.... Another sense of "comparative" literature confines it to the study of relationships between two or more literatures.

Wellek and Warren (1949: 40–41) go on to propose a third conception of Comparative Literature that identifies "with the study of literature in its totality", with "world literature", with "general" or "universal" literature.

Henry Remak (1961: 3) extended the boundaries of Comparative Literature beyond the study of literature of one particular country to

> ...the study of the relationships between literature on one hand and other areas of knowledge and belief, such as the arts (e.g. painting, sculpture, architecture, music), philosophy, history, the social sciences, (e.g. politics, economics, sociology), the sciences, religion, etc., on the other. In brief it is the comparison of one literature with another or others, and the comparison of literature with other spheres of human expression.

However, the meaning of Comparative Literature proposed by Steven Tötösy de Zepetnek seems to be the most acceptable at the present time. While accepting Remak's definition of the scope of Comparative Literature, Steven Tötösy de Zepetnek (1998: 13) expands it even further to include a political thrust to the discipline:

> In principle, the discipline of Comparative Literature is in toto a method in the study of literature in at least two ways. First, Comparative Literatures means the knowledge of more than one national language and literature, and/or it means the knowledge and application of other disciplines in and for the study of literature and second, Comparative Literature has an ideology of inclusion of the Other, be that a marginal literature in its several meanings of marginality, a genre, various text types, etc.

Coming to the Indian context, Amiya Dev emphasizes the need for translating regional language texts into English or other Indian languages in order to initiate comparative analyses. In a multilingual country like India, to know each other, to know each other's language and literature, translation is the important tool. It is through translation that one can have access to other's language, literature and culture. Amiya Dev (2011: 11) says, "...we live in a world where translation not only builds bridges but also subverts the power of dominant languages ... my cue is ... (to) stress bilingual or rather bicultural reading that may initiate comparison."

Amiya Dev also emphasizes the role of translation in building a tradition of Comparative Indian Literature. It is evident from his words that he believes that translation serves the purpose of diminishing gaps and building bridges of unity amongst various groups of people of different language and culture. Moreover, the hegemony of dominant language and literature can also be dismissed by initiating comparison between 'dominant' and 'less-powerful' language and literature. I have selected texts from different languages and cultures for my study here. It is worthwhile to mention here that the texts that I have chosen for my study do not necessarily belong to the 'canon of literary text' in the literary tradition of that particular language or culture. This is to ensure that an impartial comparison is made possible when an author of lesser reputation and his/her works are compared with an author of repute. However, the labelling of 'authors of repute' is also problematic in the sense that such categorization hardly rises above subjective judgement. Instead, this is always dependent on cultural, economic and political exigencies.

Amiya Dev believes that in a world of diverse cultures we need Comparative Literature. To talk about the relevance and importance of Comparative Literature, one is reminded of Earl Miner (1990: 238) here who says:

> The great gain from intercultural comparative study is that it avoids taking the local for the universal, the momentary for the constant, and, above all the familiar for the inevitable.

Literary scholars are of the view that literatures do not evolve in isolation from one another. From the time of the German philosopher Goethe, the necessity of World Literature has always been acknowledged. Goethe talked about 'Weltliteratur' by which he meant the memorable works of all languages. In India, Rabindranath Tagore also talked about 'Visva Sahitya' to mean the best of literatures from all the languages. Interestingly, Tagore used the English expression 'Comparative Literature' to mean World Literature.

It is true that for the study of a single literature, one does not feel obliged to study beyond his/her own language and literary tradition. But whenever two or more literatures come into contact, the need of a wider perspective is quite evident. On various occasions, in the present-day world, people come into close contact with others from different languages, cultures or literary traditions. All these "necessitated an enlargement of critical perspective" (Das, 2011: 18).

In his article 'Comparative Literature: Indian Dimension' (2011: 32), Swapan Majumdar says, "In Europe, adherence to a comparative approach was but a matter of choice, in India, it was a must, a necessity because of the multilingual state of confederacy." Satendra R. Singh says that the uniqueness of Indian literary situation demands a completely different approach. Singh (1989: 205) believes,

> No single Indian literature is complete in itself, so no study of the novels within the single language context can do justice to the genre or to the writers because of their common cultural heritage. Each novel or writer can, therefore, be properly understood only within the widest context of the Indian socio-cultural, economic, political and literary process.

While it is difficult to postulate the existence of a singular Indian literature, the study of the genre of Indian fiction definitely demands a comparative approach. To discuss Indian fiction, more specifically Indian ethnographic fiction, the comparative approach has distinct advantages over others.

Meenakshi Mukherjee (2001: 28) believes that irrespective of the language in which a novel by an Indian writer is written, it "demands direct involvement in values and experiences which are valid in the Indian context". But when we talk about values and experiences in the Indian context, very often we tend to forget that India is a vast land comprising people of different castes, religions, customs and traditions as well as of different geographical locations. This variety is bound to produce varied experiences among people/writers from different ethnic groups. Hence it is always difficult to define a single/distinct Indian situation or Indian context. Mukherjee (2001: 35) accepts that "...there is a great deal of regional variation in social structure, values and customs and problems in different parts of India, but ... the underlying situation is real to all Indians, and lies very close to their immediate experience." I believe this might be true to the Indo-Anglian fictions referred to by Mukherjee, but in case of fiction in the regional literatures, this generalization may not be applicable. The customs and rituals, the experiences of an ethnic group from North East India may be totally strange for a member of an ethnic group from South India or North India. The Assamese novel *Sava Kota Manuh* (The Man Who Slices Dead Bodies) by Yeshe Dorjee Thongchi from Arunachal Pradesh takes, for its theme, the local custom of slicing dead bodies into one hundred and eight pieces. This custom of burial might be a new or firsthand experience for the readers from other parts of India.

It needs no mention that any literature, generally speaking, can exist outside the boundaries of a single language or culture. Thus, literature has always been about bridge-building and connecting people and cultures. One of the primary objectives of Comparative Literature is to promote reading across cultural and linguistic boundaries in order to highlight everything that the exclusive focus on a so-called 'national' literature may tend to obliterate. Writers who know nothing of one another may show fascinating similarities and differences; when we read a novel by Buchi Emecheta and compare it with an Assamese novel by Lummer Dai (from Arunachal Pradesh), both with the same title, we find startling similarities and differences (Nath and Dutta, 2012). In its analysis of literature and literary traditions, Comparative Literature looks beyond and across the boundaries of single nations, languages and cultures. In doing this, it takes into account the historical, political and social realities that shape the contexts of literature.

Comparative Literature may help to re-establish the value of literary studies at a time of crisis in the humanities. The relevance of Comparative Literature, to put it very simply, is in the fact that it provides a vehicle of dialogue between cultures.

> The comparatist's effort and reward is to perceive the literary world in its fundamental unity. (Jost, 1974: xi)

Having said this, the comparatist very often finds himself in a rather strange situation in a multicultural and pluralistic setting. Charles Bernheimer, in his much discussed book *Comparative Literature in the Age of Multiculturalism* (1995: 9) points to the peculiar dilemma of the comparatist:

The more literatures you try to compare, the more like a colonizing imperialist you may seem. If you stress what these literatures have in common—thematically, morally, politically—you may be accused of imposing a universalist model that suppresses particular differences so as to foster the old humanist dream of man's worldwide similarity to man. If, on the other hand, you stress differences, then the basis of comparison becomes problematic, and your respect for the uniqueness of particular cultural formations may suggest the impossibility of any meaningful relation between cultures.

Two Approaches in Comparative Literature and the Search for Literary Universals

In their introduction to *Literary India: Comparative Studies in Aesthetics, Colonialism, and Culture*, Patrick Hogan and Lalita Pandit identify two broad ways in which a work in Comparative Literature may proceed. Firstly, it may examine literary works in parallel. This is a method that to some extent relies on the insights derived from the linguistic theories of Noam Chomsky and Joseph Greenberg. This approach "considers similarities (and to a lesser extent differences) in the properties and structures of diverse traditions focusing in particular on those properties and structures that arose independently" (Hogan and Pandit, 1995: xii). The second approach in Comparative Literature involves examination of literary works in translation. This approach "focuses on historical relations not only what one tradition has taken from another, but also what it has rejected or transformed" (Hogan and Pandit, 1995: xii).

The present study is mainly based on the parallel approach to Comparative Literature to unearth both "crosscultural constants and cultural variance" in order to develop an insight into "both our shared humanity and our cultural diversity" (Hogan and Pandit, 1995: xii). Ethnic novels in India, both by writers belonging to ethnic communities and by writers outside of these, need to be analysed as a separate tradition in itself for there are ties that bind together the ethnic communities of India.

I believe that Comparative Literature is among other things, a search for literary universals. Unfortunately today, on the few occasions when universalism finds any mention in literary criticism, it is most often denounced as a "tool of oppression" (Hogan, 1997: 224). Patrick Hogan (1997: 224) cites the example of Ashcroft, Griffiths and Tiffin who, in their influential volume *The Empire Writes Back* (2002), maintained that the notion of universality is "a hegemonic European critical tool". The Kenyan Marxist novelist Nguig wa Thiong'o became a redeeming exception to this when he proclaimed that he is "an unrepentant universalist" (quoted in Hogan, 1997: 224). Rene Wellek and Austin Warren (1949: 7) pointed out that similar to every human being, "each work of literature has its individual characteristics; but it also shares common properties with other works of art, just as every man shares traits with humanity, with all members of his sex, nation, class, profession, etc."

In his article titled 'Literary Universals' (1997: 225), Patrick Hogan draws upon Lalita Pandit's distinction between "hegemonic" and "empathic" universals to defend the concept. The distrust of literary universals, according to Pandit, arises because many "anticolonial critiques of culture equate universalism with imperialism" (1995: 207). Citing an example, she draws a distinction between Rabindranath Tagore's universalism and the imperialistic notion of universalism. Unlike Tagore, the imperialistic notion of imperialism is "nonempathic, fixed and hegemonic", expecting "to see only its own reflection in the Other", testing "the value and validity of the Other solely in terms of an already established normative self" (1995: 207). Hegemonic universals thus refer to the imposition of one set of interests on everyone, encouraging domination. Empathic universals, on the other hand, develop as "an antidote to this annihilating, nonassimilative, separatist universalism" (1995: 207).

Hogan (1997: 228) extends Pandit's argument to suggest that literary universals are those that are found in "distinct bodies of literature that do not share a common ancestor having that property or relation". With regard to literature, a theory of universals "would include a *repertoire of techniques* available to authors" (1997: 229). Techniques, for Hogan (1997: 229), include all "universal matters of form or content". My study here would limit itself to an analysis of the thematic and narrative content of the novels chosen for discussion in the search of 'literary universals'. I contend that such an approach is not opposed to the spirit of celebrating difference.

To start with, I discuss the tradition of ethnic novels in Assamese in the next chapter. In doing this, I adopt the sequential approach to make sense of the historically defined particularities of Assamese Literature. In the latter chapters, I attempt a comparative study of select Assamese novels and novels in other regional languages of India. Like Bernheimer's comparatist, I distrust "all guides that offer to decode the exotic other" and refuse "to become a detached observer exercising a free-floating, disengaged intelligence" (Bernheimer, 1995: 13). I am acutely conscious of comparative study as an ideological work in line with Steven Tötösy de Zepetnek (2005: 23) who proposed the concept of Comparative Cultural Studies in the 1980s: "the conceptualization of comparative cultural studies is a 'merger' of tenets of the discipline of comparative literature—minus the discipline's Eurocentrism and nation-orientation ... —with those of cultural studies including the latter's explicit ideological perspective."

2
The Tradition of Assamese Ethnographic Novels

Identity Politics and Linguistic Identity of Assam

When we talk of linguistic identity, very often we tend to emphasize the autonomy of a particular language. However, the fact that autonomy of a language depends more on the power associated with the language than on other factors such as syntactic or semantic features of the language, usage or script is either ignored or deliberately swept aside. In Assam, the concept of linguistic nationalism is the result of the colonial imposition of the belief that Assamese is a distorted form of the Bengali language. After the coming of the British as a result of the Yandaboo Treaty of 1826, Assam remained under the umbrella of the Bengal Presidency till the administrative reorganization of 1874. During this early phase of colonial rule, British introduced Bengali as the court language of Assam at the cost of the linguistic identity of the Assamese in 1837. The Assamese language was restored to its rightful place in 1874 (Sarma, 2009: 245).

Much of what has been happening in Assam in terms of ethnic identity politics can be traced back to the 19th century. The British kept the Ahom[1] oligarchy out from the corridors of power. With this

---

[1] The Ahoms belonged to the Shan tribe of Upper Burma, who came to Assam in 1228 and established an empire which ruled in the state for about 600 years before they were replaced by the British.

exclusion, the British set up an administrative system with the help of a migrant Bengali Hindu workforce recruited from Sylhet. It is a long-stated argument that the British tried to play a divide-and-rule policy by pitting one group/community against the other. In fact, scholars like Amalendu Guha (2006) have traced the root of present politics of conflicting identities in the region to the nineteenth century. On the other hand, the tea industry used as a workforce a group of people who were recruited from the tribal groups which mainly lived in eastern and central India. These plantation workers were then called coolies. Thus, by 1901 nearly 13 per cent of Assam's total population was born outside the state (Sharma, 2012: 79). This was a point from which the discourse of indigeneity was going to increasingly shape the history and socio-political life of Assam.

Interestingly, while the British on the one hand, encouraged the migration of 'outsiders' into Assam, they also encouraged a sort of xenophobia in the Assamese mind. The Assam Agitation[2] (1979–1985), according to Guha (2006), has its roots in the fear of the Assamese that they would one day be turned into a minority in their own land. Sanjib Baruah has a different explanation for the trajectories of the growth and emergence of ethnicity in Assam and the North East. In *India against Itself* (2001) Barua looks at the politics of colonial cartography and its impact on the Assamese. In the colonial scheme of things, Assam was no more than an extension of Bengal.

While highlighting the issues of Assamese linguistic nationalism and the subsequent phase of ethnic separatism in Assam, it is important to look at who constitutes the category of 'the Assamese'. This is obviously a very complex and sensitive issue, and there can never be a final statement of definition. After all, the Assamese identity is as much a construct as any identity is and, as such, it is subject to the

---

[2] It was a popular movement against undocumented immigrants in Assam during 1979–1985. The movement was led by All Assam Students Union (AASU) and All Assam Gana Sangram Parishad (AAGP). These groups undertook a program of protest and demonstration to compel the government to identify and expel illegal immigrants. The agitation came to an end in August 1985 following the Assam Accord , which was signed by leaders of AASU–AAGSP and Government of India. The agitation leaders formed a political party called Asom Gana Parishad. It came to power in the state of Assam in the assembly elections of 1985 and later in 1996.

same vagaries. Notions of identity are bound to change across time and space. What it means to be an Assamese for a highly educated middle-class person living in a metropolitan set-up is obviously going to be different from the understanding of Assamese-ness of a person living elsewhere. However, we can, for the present, accept a broad definition of the category of 'the Assamese' taking features of general acceptance. First, the term 'Assamese' is used to refer to the people for whom Assam is their 'real' or 'imagined' homeland. Second, besides this territorial identity, the word 'Assamese' denotes the group of people who speak 'Asamiya' (Assamese language). When we say 'Asamiya-speaking people', we presume that this includes two groups: (a) one is the group of people whose mother tongue is Assamese, and (b) another is the group of people whose mother tongue is not Assamese but have acquired Assamese language formally or informally. When we refer to all the people residing in the Assam, it is inclusive of the *bhumiputras* (autochtones) of *Assam* (a term used during and after the Assam Accord[3] of 1985 to refer to the indigenous inhabitants of Assam) and the 'ethnic Assamese community' and also the Muslims and Hindu Bengalis, Marwaris and other minority migrant groups, tribals and adivasis.

If we agree to this wider definition of 'Assamese', we have to accept that Assam is the homeland of people from different ethnic groups who speak different languages. Therefore, to talk about Assamese linguistic identity is to embrace the accommodative nature of the Assamese language. In the past, there was no conscious attempt on the part of the people from the indigenous tribal groups residing in Assam to communicate in any language other than Assamese. As such, people from different ethnic groups outside the narrow group of the 'ethnic Assamese' accepted Assamese as a medium to express their creative thoughts. Moreover, there was an earnest attempt on the part of the middle-class Assamese people (in its broader sense) to fight against the colonial dictum that Assamese is a broken form of the Bengali

---

[3] It was a Memorandum of Settlement (MoS) signed between representatives of the Government of India and the leaders of the Assam movement in New Delhi on 15 August 1985. The accord brought an end to the Assam Agitation and paved the way for the leaders of the agitation to form a political party that formed a government in the state of Assam in 1985.

language. In its attempt to prove that Assamese is an independent language, the people of Assam tried to establish an Assamese linguistic tradition irrespective of their own ethnic identities. I believe that the creative writings of the authors from indigenous ethnic people like Rong Bong Terang, Khagen Pegu, and so on, are the results of the vision of 'greater Assam' of social thinkers like Bishnu Rabha and Bhupen Hazarika and even Lummer Dai.

But, in 1960, during the Bimala Prasad Chaliha government, the Assam (Official) Language Act (ALA) was passed granting Assamese the status of the sole official language of the state. The ALA started to arouse violent communal clashes among the people of the state due to the multilingual character of Assam. Though these communal clashes started initially among the Bengali and the Assamese communities, in the later years these clashes started to spread to other indigenous ethnic groups of the state.

Therefore, we observe a perceivable change in the writings from the indigenous ethnic writers both in the medium of writing as well as in the subject matter. Writers of the earlier generation considered Assamese as their mother tongue (I have discussed Lummer Dai in a separate section) and also acquired Assamese as their first language. They were happy to express themselves in a language (Assamese) which was known by the majority of the people (I have quoted Yeshe Dorjee Thongchi in a later chapter). However, the declaration of the ALA and the perceived hegemony of the 'ethnic Assamese' widened the gap between them and the ethnic minorities. One result of this was that the new generation of the ethnic minorities felt gradually cut off from the Assamese language. Thus, it is probably not a surprise that we see few creative writers in Assamese coming out of the new generation of indigenous ethnic writers.

A Brief Overview of Assamese Literature

Assamese literature has a long and glorious history starting with the Charyapadas, which were Buddhist devotional songs written between 8th and 12th century AD. While the Charyapadas existed in both oral and written forms, the starting point of written Assamese Literature is generally considered to be Hem Saraswati's *Prahlada Charita* written in the late 13th century. The most well-known poet of the Pre-Vaishnavite period of Assam was Madhav Kandali, who rendered Valmiki's *Ramayana* into Assamese verse (*Kotha Ramayana*, 14th century) under the patronage of Mahamanikya, a Kachari king of Jayantapura. Madhav Kandali's *Ramayana* is stated to be the first of its kind amongst all the regional languages of northern and eastern India. Rudra Kandali's translation of *Drona Parva* of *The Mahabharata* appeared in the 14th century. In the 15th century, Sankardeva, the great patron of the Vaishnavite movement in Assam, emerged as the doyen of Assamese literature. Along with his disciple, Madhavdeva, Sankardeva enriched Assamese literature and culture with *borgeet* (devotional songs), *ankiya nat* and *bhaona* (traditional Assamese play and theatre) and many other religious and spiritual writings. With Bhattadeva's *Katha Gita* (Assamese version of *The Gita*), Assam can also boast of the oldest writing in prose in the whole of north India.

The modern Assamese period began with the publication of the *Bible* in Assamese prose by the American Baptist Missionaries in 1813. Assamese Literature flowered in the 19th century with writers like Anandaram Dhekial Phukan, Gunabhiram Barua, Nathan Brown, Miles Bronson and Hemachandra Barua. Published towards the end of the 19th century, Padmanath Gohain Baruah's *Bhanumoti* (1892) is considered to be the first Assamese novel. However, there was an already existent tradition of fiction writing in Assam even before this. Hemchandra Barua's *Bahire Rong Chong Bhitore Kuwa Bhaturi* (Colourful Outside, Empty Inside) had the semblance of a modern novel. Padmavati Devi Phukononi's *Sudhormar Upakhyan* (The Tale of Sudharma, 1884) can be considered to be a precursor of the modern Assamese novel. Besides, even before this, quite a few works of translation were undertaken by the editors of *Orunodoi* (The Rise of the Sun, 1846), the first Assamese magazine, and other British missionaries. The first editors of *Orunodoi*, Nathan Brown and Dan Forth, started the serial publication of the Assamese translation of John Bunyan's *The Piligrim's Progress* titled *Jatrikor Jatra* in 1848. Though there is some confusion about the origin of the two novels associated with Reverend A.K. Gurney, a British missionary—*Kaminikanta* (1877) and *Alyokeshi*

Beshyar Bishay (The Case of Alokeshi, the Prostitute, 1877)—these are generally believed to have been translated from Bengali. Mrs Gurney translated *Phulmoni aru Karuna* (Phulmoni and Karuna) from Bengali in 1877.

The period of Assamese modern literature began with the publication of the Assamese journal *Jonaki* (Moonlight, 1889), in which Lakshminath Bezbaroa introduced the genre of short story in Assamese. Thus began the *Jonaki* period of Assamese literature which was made significant by the contributions of Chandrakumar Agarwalla, Hemchandra Goswami and Lakshminath Bezbaroa. Modern Assamese literature has been enriched by the works of Jyoti Prasad Agarwalla, Hem Barua, Atul Chandra Hazarika, Nalini Bala Devi, Navakanta Barua, and others. Today, Assam boasts of a large number of writers who have helped to secure firmly the position of Assamese literature in the national scenario. In addition to numerous writers being awarded the prestigious Sahitya Akademi award, Birendra Kumar Bhattacharjya and Indira Goswami have earned the Jnanpith award, the highest literary award conferred in India.

While there is a long-established tradition of writers in Assam, there is no such tradition of ethnographic writers or ethnographic fictions as yet. Writers in Assam, as elsewhere, have dealt with numerous themes and subject matters in their fictional works. Many writers have made significant contributions to the growth and development of Assamese literature with materials from the ethnic world. It is significant to note here that many writers from different parts of North East India (who are members of an ethnic community) write in Assamese. They talk about the ethnic societies in a language which is not their own. Moreover, many writers (in Assam) outside the ethnic community also write fictions taking materials from the ethnic community. In my study here, I would be taking up fictions written with materials from ethnic societies irrespective of the author's background.

Since Bengal was the first region to come in close contact with the British, the earliest Indian novels came to be written in Bengali. The first few attempts consisted of sketches of contemporary Bengali society, but the new genre really became established with the form of historical novel. It is interesting to note that the novel emerged at different times in different regions of India, but almost everywhere the first crop showed a preoccupation with historical romance. In fact, the full development of the Indian novel as a whole may be divided into three large stages: (a) historical romance, (b) social or political realism, and (c) psychological novels showing an introspective concern with the individual. In most Indian languages, the developments occurred in this order, although not simultaneously (Mukherjee, 2001: 30).

In spite of its rise to prominence, the concept of the 'ethnic novel' as a distinct genre continues to be a matter of controversy. In a very general sense, the novels that represent the life and society of minority ethnic communities may be categorized as 'ethnic'. In a more limited sense, novels based on any traditional ethnic custom may also be categorized as ethnic. It is problematic to state categorically whether 'ethnic novels' should include only those works of fiction that have been written by writers belonging to ethnic communities or should also include any work of an ethnographic nature, independent of the writer's cultural background. Thus, the matter of contention is in deciding whether ethnicity in fiction is to be defined in terms of the characters, settings and the societies that are represented or in terms of the writer's ethnic or cultural identity. In this situation, one is reminded of the slightly different context of Sherry Simon's description of the 'cultural turn' in translation studies:

> ..."culture" is recognized as one of the most difficult and overdetermined concepts in the contemporary human and social sciences ... [translators] must understand the culture of the original text, because texts are "embedded" in a culture. The more extensive is this "embedding," the more difficult it will be to find equivalents for terms and ideas .... The difficulty with such statements is that they seem to presume a unified cultural field which the term inhabits; the translator must simply track down the precise location of the term within it and then investigate the corresponding cultural field for corresponding realities. What this image does not convey is the very difficulty of determining "cultural meaning." This meaning is not located within the culture itself but in the process of negotiation which is part of its continual reactivation. (1996: 130)

Kirin Narayan in her very important essay 'How Native Is a "Native" Anthropologist?' (1993: 671–672) problematizes the simplified and neat distinction between 'native' and 'non-native' anthropologists. This, I believe, applies equally well to the distinction between writers who wear the tag of 'cultural insiders' and those who are labelled as 'cultural outsiders':

> Instead of the paradigm emphasizing a dichotomy between outsider/insider or observer/observed, I propose that at this historical moment we might more profitably view each [writer] in terms of shifting identifications amid a field of interpenetrating communities and power relations. The loci along which we are aligned with or set apart from those whom we study are multiple and in flux.

In my study, I propose to include the novels of the writers who have portrayed the lives and societies of the ethnic communities of India. In this chapter, I will focus on select Assamese ethnic novels representing the tribes of North East India. Select novels depicting the rites and rituals, customs and traditions of any minority ethnic community of the North East, written either by a writer 'belonging' to that community or 'outside' it, will come under the purview of my study. I will begin by tracing the history of Assamese ethnic novels from the beginning till date. I will also use the term 'ethnographic fiction' to refer to these works to stress their representation of lived reality. I would, however, like to qualify the term by saying that not all the fictional works that I will be dealing with were necessarily the result of the writers' fieldwork.

Critics like Arnold Krupat (1992) have discussed ethnography as an order of literature. Talking about the relationship between fiction and ethnography, Kirin Narayan (1999: 143) says,

> In ethnography, the use of fictional devices like suspense, particularity, and close attention to the surface manifestations of subjective states has the potential to make for richer, more nuanced, evocative, and readable texts. Simultaneously, for fiction, a solid if implied sense of what C. Wright Mills calls "the sociological imagination"—that is, how larger structural forces shape the most intimate details of personal lives—may potentially make for more powerful and engaged creations.

James Clifford (1986a: 6) too, says,

> Ethnographic writings can properly be called fictions in the sense of 'something made or fashioned', the principle burden of the word's Latin root

fingere. But it is important to preserve the meaning not merely of making, but also of making up, of inventing things not actually real.

Having said this, it must be admitted that ethnographic fiction is primarily fiction and not ethnography. The most significant difference between ethnography and fiction is that while reading ethnography, readers take it for granted that they are being offered 'facts' and while reading fiction they assume that the narrated events need not necessarily be real. It is another matter that 'facts' are not necessarily neutral, if not in any other way, at least in terms of their selection by the author. And in this sense, it would be foolhardy to assume that literary facts bear a 'direct' or 'factual' relationship with reality. To quote from another essay by James Clifford (1986b: 98) in which his description of ethnographic writing applies as well to ethnographic or ethnic fiction: "these stories simultaneously describe real cultural events and make additional, moral, ideological, and even cosmological statements."

Furthermore,

> The meanings of an ethnographic account are uncontrollable. Neither an author's intention, nor the disciplinary writing, nor the rules of genre can limit the readings of a text that will emerge with new historical, scientific, or political projects. (Clifford, 1986b: 120)

Charles Bernheimer (1995: 8) remarked in a similar vein:

> A literary work can never authentically mirror a culture not only because that culture is not at one with itself but also because the work is a literary representation and hence not a transparent medium but a formal structure. Furthermore, the criterion of authenticity tends to equalize all cultures in a relativist haze and thereby destroys any possibility of differential judgment and comparison.

I will begin with a brief introductory discussion of the novels in a chronological order. In addition, I will make a division of the ethnic Assamese novels depending on the authorship (cultural identity of the authors) of these novels. The ethnic novels which are written by 'insiders' (members of that particular community) and the ethnic novels written by 'outsiders' (members outside that community) will be discussed separately in this chapter. I will conclude the chapter with a comparative analysis of two novels written by a cultural 'insider' and a cultural 'outsider'. The tradition of the Assamese ethnic novel is intimately linked to the rise of the Assamese novel in general. Moreover, it is pertinent to keep in mind that, conventionally, the Assamese ethnic novel has hardly been credited with having a tradition of its own.

The six-century long reign of the Ahoms was brought to an end by three rounds of invasion by the Burmese army who were then pushed back by the forces of British East India Company, thereby paving the way to the surrender of the region to the company. Subsequent to the signing of the treaty of Yandaboo in 1826, the British imposed Bengali as a medium of instruction in schools and courts across Assam in 1836. Following a sustained campaign, Assamese was reinstated in 1873 as the state language. As mentioned earlier, in 1848, Dr Nathan Brown and Dan Forth serialized the Assamese translation of John Bunyan's *Pilgrims' Progress* in *Orunodoi* (the first periodical of Assamese) with the title *Jatrikor Jatra*. Though falling short of the structural form of a full-fledged novel, it did present the first taste of a novel for Assamese readers. It was published in a book-form in 1857. In 1854, Mrs Gurney translated a Bengali novel into Assamese as *Phulmoni aru Karuna*. Then in 1877, *Kaminikanta* by A.K. Gurney, the first 'original novel' in Assamese, was published from the Baptist Mission Press in Sivasagar. A.K. Gurney's *Alyokeshi Beshyar Bishay* was also published in the same year. All these 'novels' highlighted religious issues, but through these, as Maheswar Neog (2010:196) says, Assamese readers were introduced to the aesthetic beauty of the novel as an art form.

A year after the publication of the Assamese journal *Jonaki*, another journal *Bijuli* (Lightning, 1890) came into being and it was in the pages of *Bijuli*, in the early 1890s, that the first proper Assamese novel *Bhanumati* by Padamanath Gohain Baruah was serialized. The following year his second novel *Lahori* was published in a book form. In 1894, Rajanikanta Bordoloi published his first novel *Miri Jiyori* (The Mising Damsel). Set against the backdrop of the Mising tribe of Assam, it is a tragic love story and is considered to be the first Assamese social novel.

It is significant that chronologically *Miri Jiyori* is the third Assamese novel and through it the writer tries to portray the worldview and the society of the ethnic Mising community of the Brahmaputra valley. For a modern-day reader, certain aspects of *Miri Jiyori* might seem on the one hand to be undemocratic, and on the other hand, to be presenting too romanticized a picture of the stereotypically 'naïve' and 'simple' tribe. However, a novel such as *Miri Jiyori* needs to be contextualized and seen as the product of a specific historical moment. It is undeniable that *Miri Jiyori* is a historically important literary text in more ways than one. At a point of time when no other writer from Assam ever thought of straining his eyes beyond the caste Hindu community, Bordoloi tried to represent the society of the Misings through fiction. In this sense alone, if nothing else, Bordoloi breaks new grounds. In spite of being a cultural 'outsider' to the Mising tribe, Bordoloi was "a careful but distant observer, a charmed spectator of the tribal society" (Sarma, 2010).

Following Rajanikanta Bordoloi, there appears a group of writers, both from ethnic communities and 'outside', who depict the lives and societies of the ethnic people of the North East. I will discuss these writers in two separate sections. I will first take a look at the novels of those writers of ethnographic novels who do not belong to any ethnic community.

Prafulla Dutta Goswami's *Kecha Patar Kapani* (The Tremor of the Green Leaves, 1952) presents, in part, a picture of ethnic life. In this novel, the character of Robin Kumar is apparently modelled on the legendary figure of Bishnu Rabha. This character is shown as a medium through which socialism percolates down to the Bodo-Kachari community. The problems faced by this community along with its rituals are very well depicted in the novel.

Navakanta Barua's *Kapilipariya Sadhu* (The Story by the Side of the Kapili River, 1953) is set against the background of the freedom movement in India. The protagonist is a member of an ethnic group from the undivided Nagaon District. Through this character, the writer tries to express the "simplicity, obstinacy, devotion and emotional nature of the ethnic community" (Bora, 2000: 129; my translation). On one hand, the novel expresses the exploitation, deception and trickery of the urban middle-class Hindu when it comes to their treatment of the ethnic minorities of the state. But it also shows the honest urge in some of them to genuinely contribute to the development of these ethnic groups.

It was in 1955 that the first Assamese novel set against the background of the tea-garden labourers was published. Written by Jogesh Das, the novel was titled *Dawar aru Nai* (Clouds Have Gone). Though the threat of war always looms large in the background, the novel does not present a direct description of war. Instead, Das explores life in the Chukeriting Tea Garden near Doomdoma town. The hassle-free and easygoing life in the tea garden along with the pain, sorrow and dreams of the tribes are very well depicted in this novel. The novel presents a description of the exploitation of tea-garden labourers and the ill-treatment meted out to them by the members of so-called upper-caste urban society. The attitude of the upper caste towards the tribe is subjected to a very close scrutiny through the character of Girin.

Birinchi Kumar Baruah's *Seuji Patar Kahini* (The Story of the Green Leaves) was published in 1959, with the writer using the pen name Rasna Baruah. In it Baruah gives a picture of the pre-Independence Assamese society as a whole and the tea-garden community in particular. Baruah takes pains to depict the Machiavellian colonial policy of 'divide and rule'. Through the character of Sonia, the novelist tries to show the resistance to the cruelty and exploitation meted out to the tea-garden community. The novelist reveals a deep sense of attachment to the people while presenting their plight and sufferings.

Kailash Sarma stretched his eyes to the hill tribes in his novels and presented the Naga tribe in his novels in the time-period between 1950 and 1960. All the three novels of Kailash Sarma—*Bidrohi Nagar Hatat* (In the Hands of the Naga Rebels), *Anami Nagini* (The Nameless Naga Girl) and *Dalimir Xapon* (The Dreams of Dalimi)—are based on the Naga society. In *Bidrohi Nagar Hatat*, he brings the Naga society, along with the Naga agitation, to the fore. Kandarpa, the protagonist, is a boy from the plains. He goes to the Naga Hills to earn his livelihood and is trapped in the hands of the Naga rebels. He falls in love with a Naga girl, Nikula, but later leaves her with the assurance that he would marry her. However, as it turns out, he is in love with Chizeva, the nurse, as well. Finally, he marries neither of them and escapes from the Naga Hills. Kandarpa lives in the midst of the Naga rebels but never tries to understand the problems and difficulties of the Nagas. He works for them just to ensure his own safety. Kandarpa's outlook is representative of the plains people's attitude towards the hill tribes in general. Apparently, Kandarpa seems to understand the sincerity and devotion of the rebels, and he talks very highly of their self-sacrifice, but at the same time he says that the principles and the ideals of the rebels are just some utopian goals which are impossible to achieve.

Another novel by the same author titled *Anami Nagini* (1963) is about the changes in the life of a non-Christian girl, Jasmi, under the influence of a Christian girl called Methy. Breaking away from her engagement with a boy, she falls in love with a Christian youth called Joseph. After Joseph's death, she is thrown into distress not only because of an emotional breakdown but also due to worldly disadvantages. With this novel, the novelist tries to present the life and society of the Angami Nagas. Different aspects of the Naga life are being portrayed here. However, the lack of any particular issues related to the Naga life and their problems and sufferings makes it questionable whether the novel can be seen to have done enough justice to the ethnic world of the Nagas.

The third novel by Kailash Sarma, *Dalimir Sopon* was published in 1972. Here he tries to portray the life of the soldier against the background of the Naga revolution. Though he tries to depict the Naga way of life in this novel, he seems to be ignorant of the practical and complex issues related to it. His love for the Naga Hills and for the people living there, in no way, helps him to support their revolution. He discards its very idea. Perhaps the writer's Gandhian ideology prevents him from expressing his support for any revolution that turns violent. Nevertheless, *Dalimir Sopon* does introduce the readers to the socially relevant issues related to the life of the Nagas through the medium of fiction.

An immensely important name in the field of Assamese ethnographic fiction is Birendrakumar Bhattacharjee, the first recipient of the Jnanpith Award from Assam. His novel *Iyaruingom* was published in 1960. Much later, the novelist himself translated it into English as *Love in the Time of Insurgency*. This novel is written against the backdrop of Naga life. The story is based on the Tankhul Naga tribe residing in Manipur and their sufferings during the separatist movement led by Phizo. The story goes back to the last few years of the Second World War (few years prior to the independence of India) when the Japanese troops were retreating from parts of Manipur and the Naga hills.

The novelist portrays a vivid picture of the Naga Hills in terms of the natural landscape and the lives and rituals as well as the hopes and aspirations of its people. Almost all the major characters of the novel like Richang, Sarengla, Khutingla are from the Naga society and so their activities, hopes and aspirations are definitely linked to the Naga way of life.

Birendrakumar Bhattacharjee's *Mrityunjaya* (Conquering Death) presents a fresh perspective in terms of its presentation of an ethnic world. Dimi is the main character of the novel. Though written against the background of the freedom movement, several pages of the novel are full of descriptions of the Wangala festival[4] of the Garos. The novelist does not make any attempt to hide his sympathy for the status of women in this society. At the same time, the novel presents the social ethos, the caste system, customs and traditions of the Garo society.

In 1965, Pashupati Bharadwaj's novel *Simsangar Dutipar* (The Two Sides of the Simsang River) was published. Garo life and rituals are pictured in this novel. It describes the plight, pain and sufferings of the Garo community of the Mymensingh district of East Pakistan after the partition of India. The novelist's main concern is the horrifying socio-political situation created by the partition of the country. The novel is about human suffering and pain. However, the readers are not introduced to the core problems of the ethnic community of the Garos.

Amulya Barua wrote *Ukhun Jangha* (My Treasure) based on the Khasi lifeworld in 1973. The protagonist of the novel is a Khasi child who is interested in the egg of a hen that he discovers in a nest. Wanglam, the child is obsessed with the chick that comes out from the egg. His mother gives a name to the chick—Ukhun Jangha. Wanglam's imaginary world, as well as his day-to-day life, revolves around Ukhun Jangha. But his father is incapable of appreciating the emotions and passions associated with such a tiny creature of God. Wanglam's father, being squeezed by poor economic condition and under the intoxicating effect of wine, is depicted as a character devoid

---

[4] Wangala is a festival celebrated by the Garo tribe living in the states of Meghalaya and Assam in India and in some parts of Bangladesh. It is a harvest festival. They give thanks to the God and Goddess, called Misi Saljong (Sun-God), for blessing the people with a rich harvest. Wangala is celebrated in the months from September to December.

of emotions. Unable to appreciate the feelings of his son, he kills the chick. His son, Wanglam, is terribly hurt by this, and it leads to his death following a spell of high fever. The novelist tries to highlight certain sensitive issues relating to child psychology, and he does so by drawing a picture of the dull mundane life of the people living in the coal mines. This society is deprived of the joys of living, and the emotions and feelings of its inhabitants are repressed by the structures of society. The matrilineal Khasi society with its songs and dances, and rites and ritual is well represented here.

Jadav Phukan wrote two novels based on the ethnic life of the Karbi people. *Mekroki* was published in 1982 while *Kengwat Kasedong* (Walking on One's Footprints) was published in 1989. *Mekroki* is about Mekroki, a Karbi girl who has to suffer a lot due to the rigid hold of tribal traditions and rituals. In addition to reflecting the conflict between tradition and modernity, the novel is replete with ancient traditional beliefs and customs of the Karbi society.

In *Kengwat Kasedong*, the novelist introduces different aspects of the Karbi society. The Karbi youth, Dikay Engti, is the protagonist who learns the skill of repairing cars in the plains. Coming close to the plains people and their lifestyles he starts to imitate them. He develops a love affair with Lily Engti from his own sub-tribe (which is not permissible in the Karbi society) because of which he has to face social castigation. To foreground the practices of customary law, the novelist talks about different ancient customs and traditional beliefs of this ethnic society. The descriptions of *jhum* cultivation and *samangkang* dance-form of the Karbis are presented here.

In 1996, Dhrubajyoti Bora's novel *Simantar Sur* (Tunes from the Border) was published. The novel is set against the backdrop of the Arunachalee society. Without any conventional protagonists, the novel presents different aspects of the lives of diverse ethnic groups of Arunachal Pradesh. There are detailed descriptions of the customs and traditions, beliefs and superstitions of different tribes of the state in this novel. The rites and rituals associated with birth, death and marriage, and the description of various festivals are presented. While presenting the glorious aspects of the lives of the ethnic communities of the state, the novelist tries to overcome the tendency of non-ethnic writers to look at ethnic communities from an outsider's perspective or from the position of someone belonging to more 'developed' societies.

Sarna Bora is an important name in the field of Assamese ethnographic fiction who wrote a few novels based on the ethnic societies of Assam. Her *Simsang Nadir Hanhi* (The Smile of the Simsang River, 1987) and *Diyung Nadir Geet* (The Song of the Diyung River, 1986) are based on the Garo and Dimasa lives and societies. The novelist tries to bring about a sense of unity among different communities, ethnic or non-ethnic. Her urge for unity and integration leads her to bring together characters from different communities. In *Diyung Nadir Geet*, Dhanjit is offered financial help by his Muslim friend, Rahmat Ali, at the time of dire need. Again, Rahmat Ali's son gives company to Dhanjit's mother who is alone at home. Dhanjit goes to the hills and falls in love with Rupashi, the daughter of Gobind Fanglu. She marries Dhanjit and comes to the plains, and gets adjusted there with the lifestyles of the plains people. There is no particular issue relating to any ethnic community that the novelist tries to address. Instead, she tries to picture the world in front of her in the hope of bringing together various groups of people.

In *Simsang Nadir Hanhi*, she takes the Garo society as the background of her novel. But the central character of the novel is a boy from the plains. Dr Dev Choudhury, though not from the ethnic community of the Garos, wants to live his life in the midst of them. The novel showcases the traditional Garo society in terms of its beliefs and customs. Worship of the evil spirit for recovery from diseases is a common practice in this world. Dr Dev Choudhury tries to apply modern scientific medicines to cure the afflicted. The writer tries to convey the message of social reform through the character of the doctor. The age-old customs, beliefs and superstitions of the traditional Garo society are represented in the novel, and the doctor is portrayed as a means to reform the darker side of these beliefs.

Though in Prafulla Dutta Goswami's *Kecha Patar Kapani* and Medini Choudhury's *Ferenggadaw*, the life and society of the Bodos are described to some extent, these two novels are not representative of ethnic life. In *Ferenggadaw,* the novel based on the life of the legendary figure Bishnu Rabha, some issues related to Bodo life are mentioned but no specific issues concerning their lives and societies are dealt with by the novelist. In 1992, Umakanta Sarma wrote a novel *Bharand Pakhir Jak* (A Flock of Vulture-type Birds) where he introduces relevant issues related to the question of ethnic identity of the Bodos. In this novel, the novelist describes the eviction of the ethnic communities and the lack of attention from the government on this issue. At the same time the novelist talks of assimilation. He says division is a political process. It is not a social issue. A reading of the novel reveals the writer's unmistakable association with the problems of the Bodos.

In his *Ejak Manuh Ekhan Aranya* (A Herd of People, A Forest; 1986), Umakanta Sarma portrays the lives of the tea-garden labourers. He depicts the sad story of the journey of the labourers from their native places to the tea gardens of Assam. Though he tries to present the socio-economic situations and mental condition of the labourers, he is unable to portray the exploitation meted out to these people.

More recently, some writers have tried to look at the ethnic worlds of the North East from fresh perspectives. Bikashjyoti Baruah depicts the life of the ethnic people of Arunachal Pradesh in his novel *Pahari Kanya* (Daughter of the Hills, 2006). The novel reveals details about different places and ideas associated with the ethnic people of Arunachal Pradesh. From that point of view, *Pahari Kanya* fits into the genre of Assamese ethnographic fiction.

In his book *Tribals in Indian English Novel* (2008: 12), A.K. Chaturvedi says,

> Portrayal of the tribals in ancient Indian literature shows contradiction in the treatment meted out to them. Some incidents show that they were given very fair treatment and were in no way discriminated against while other incidents show that they were looked down upon and were very unjustly treated by the upper strata of society.

We can read this statement as applicable to the literature of modern India too. While talking about the depiction of ethnic worlds in literature, we need to consider who is representing whom and from what vantage point. I have already discussed those Assamese novels which represent ethnic lives and societies written by non-ethnic writers. I shall now look at those ethnographic novels which have been written by writers belonging to various ethnic communities and who are therefore conventionally considered to be 'cultural insiders' of those communities.

Lummer Dai (1940–2002) and Yeshe Dorjee Thongchi (1952–) are two pioneering litterateurs of Arunachal Pradesh. They introduce the readers to the life and society of Arunachal Pradesh in all its variety. The ethnic, cultural and traditional varieties of the state are best reflected in the literary works of these writers. For an anthropologist or for a curious ethnographer, it is possible to look at the tribal culture like an "alien gazer" who might see the "strange and exotic aspect" of it (Misra, 2001: 33). But a person, who is fortunate to be both an insider as well as a creative writer, can write with the perspective of one who constitutes an integral part of that very culture.

Both Dai and Thongchi belong to tribal communities of Arunachal Pradesh and they could not receive education in their respective mother tongues and, therefore, they wrote in Assamese, the language that was the medium of instruction in the educational institutes of Arunachal Pradesh till 1971 (Chowdhury, 1983: 315). Moreover, Assamese was used as a link language among different tribes as very often the language of one tribe is not comprehensible to another. Assamese was widely used in meetings, public gatherings and marketplaces by different communities of the state as a lingua franca.

Dai and Thongchi have cited different reasons for the selection of the Assamese language for their writings. Lummer Dai's nephew, Kaling Borang (2006: 4), says:

> ...Assamese teachers were the pioneers who taught in schools even in far-flung areas.... They felt at home in NEFA as it was a part of the once undivided Assam.... They were devoted and dedicated to their duties with heart and soul.... Therefore, the pioneer teachers are still remembered by many senior officials with gratitude and reverence. Lummer Dai is one example of students taught by those pioneering dedicated Assamese teachers.

As Assamese was the medium of instruction right from the level of primary school education, it was quite close to being the mother tongue of the Arunachalese. In an interview with Ajanta Dutta, Lummer Dai says, "I think that mother tongue is the best medium to express one's feelings. Assamese is not my mother tongue. But I have an association with the Assamese language since the time I was being suckled by my mother" (*Aaji*, 3 February 2002; my translation).

Similarly, Yeshe Dorjee Thongchi has said that the chief reason behind his choice of the Assamese language for his writings was the fact that he was taught in Assamese medium from the days of his primary school education. In an interview with Girin Tamuli and R.N. Koley (2006: 44), he says:

> ...I had a personal liking for the [Assamese] language. From a practical point of view, Assamese is the language which is accessible to the majority of our people. People coming down from the hills to the plains interact, exchange views and feelings through the Assamese language.

One could also argue that Lummer Dai and Yeshe Dorjee Thongchi chose to write in the relatively well-established literary tradition of Assamese. Further, writing in Assamese grants them a wider readership than writing in their mother tongues would possibly have had. Lummer Dai's published novels are *Paharar Xile Xile* (In the Midst of the Hills, 1961), *Prithivir Hanhi* (Laughter of the Earth, 1963), *Mon aru Mon* (Different Minds, 1967), *Kanyar Mulya* (Bride Price, 1978) and *Upar Mahal* (Higher Levels, 2003). Dai's novels (except the last one, *Upar Mahal*) are somehow related to the traditional social life of the Adis. Dai depicts the rituals, beliefs and social practices of the Adi community in his novels. In fact, an insider's view of the life and community of the Adis can be seen through his novels. Each of his novels can be examined from various perspectives as these works shed light on a diverse range of themes. The themes of love and betrayal, pain and conflict (both internal and external), social customs, conflict between generations as well as the social transformations taking place in the modern society of Arunachal—all these are the concerns and preoccupations of Lummer Dai in his novels.

Lummer Dai's *Paharar Xile Xile* (1961) is considered to be the first novel written about the tribal people of Arunachal by an Arunachalee. In *Paharar Xile Xile,* Dai attempts to look at the position of women in society. He talks of the love, suffering and anguish that the protagonist Bati experiences. Bati is compared by the author to a wild flower which, though not nurtured, spreads its smell all around. He has said that women like Bati, who are utterly deprived of the advantages of modern civilization, are not rare in society (Preface to *Paharar Xile Xile*). Moreover, the practice of 'slavery' is another important theme of the novel. In a sense the story of the novel revolves around this theme. The writer mentions in the Preface that though 'slavery' has been abolished in the Adi society, one who is born of a slave woman is still considered to belong to the lower class. There are impediments in the way of inter-class marriages in the society. The novel is set against rural life and, therefore, Dai is able to look at traditional beliefs and social customs. There is also a sense of protest against the prevalent evils of society along with the clash between two generations. *Paharar Xile Xile* is a novel about love and separation, jealousy and torture (both physical and mental), and above all, a story of a young couple who has to suffer a lot due to the cruel system of slavery. The novel was written in the 1950s and depicts the Arunachalee society of the time when slavery was still prevalent.

Prithivir Hanhi (1963) begins with a vivid description of a *mosup* and an Adi village. This novel, like the other novels we have discussed, has many references to Adi social life, including the Etoro and Solung festivals, *delong* dance and *kebang*. There are descriptions of the *ponung* dance, particularly the dance of girls dressed in male costumes. The Etoro festival is celebrated in the *mosup* of the village, and the *miri* (priest) initiates it by chanting the mantras. He sings about the myth of origin of the world and its creatures, and the youths of the *mosup* move and dance around it together. Dai has elaborately described the Etoro festival and the rituals associated to it in this novel. There is a long reference to a song sung in the *delong* dance (Dai, 1963: 97–98). Even as the story progresses smoothly, there is mention of the varied rituals, beliefs and practices of Adi society. The novel also shows the transformations taking place in the society and raises questions regarding the authenticity of *kebang* and people's protest against the unfairness that has crept into it. Satyendranath Sarma (1976: 245; my translation) says, "The novelist does not shy away from exposing the faults in *kebang* or criticizing it."

The major thematic concern of *Mon aru Mon* (1967) is the deep unselfish love of Gidum (a widow) for a dog that she does not consider to be just an animal but a being with human qualities and emotions.

The old widow comes to have a very close relation with the dog after the passing away of her family members. The dog is no less than a loving relative to grandmother Gidum. In fact, at the end of the novel, we are left wondering whether Gidum or the Bomong, the dog, is the real protagonist of the novel. The novel talks more about the dog, its activities and behaviour, its loyalty and finally, its death followed by that of Gidum. *Mon aru Mon* is really a wonderful addition to the oeuvre of Assamese literature. The presentation of a dog as one of the central characters of the novel was a brilliant addition to the Assamese novel.

Lummer Dai received the Sitanath Brahma Choudhuri award from the Assam Sahitya Sabha for *Kanyar Mulya* (1978) which undoubtedly is his most critically acclaimed novel. *Kanyar Mulya* depicts the Adi social life through its presentation of one of the oldest social institutions of human society—marriage. The protagonist Gumba is the victim of the long-established tradition of the Adis—the social practice of taking and giving bride price. As the title indicates, it is clear that the novel is about the then prevalent social custom of bride price in the Adi community. According to the social custom of the Adis as shown in Dai's novel, the marriage of a girl is fixed at an early age, sometimes just after birth, taking the price of the bride from the groom's family.

In *Kanyar Mulya*, when Gumba is still a little child, her father Kargum enters into an agreement with Mindak, according to which after a certain period of time, Gumba will have to go to Mindak's house as his daughter-in-law (as the wife of his son, Dakat). Gumba protests against it. Even when faced with the impending threat of death, Gumba does not give up her protest against the long-established system of child marriage. Kargum, her father, is of course a representative of the old generation who strictly adheres to the age-old traditions, social practices and beliefs but dwells in conflict between his love, care and sense of duty for his daughter and his sense of responsibility towards the society. When examined thoroughly, *Kanyar Mulya* will enclose varieties of different ideas and themes that the writer tries to focus on.

Upar Mahal (2003) is quite different in manner and subject matter from Dai's other novels. In all his previously written novels, he has dealt with the Adis and their social life, their customs and rituals, traditions and beliefs. Here, we see a totally different picture of the new generation—a picture of the Arunachalee society in general.

The transformation taking place in the society of Arunachal Pradesh, a society comprising different tribes as well as people from the plains, is the main focus of the novel. In *Upar Mahal*, there is mention of different customs and traditions, rituals and cultures of different tribes of Arunachal Pradesh, but the author soars over artistic heights in vividly showing the rapid social transformation taking place in the society. The young lot with their new values and the beliefs of a money- and power-driven society can be seen reflected in different characters and in their dialogues and actions. In almost all his previous novels, the author has presented people who are simple by nature, untouched and as yet unspoiled by the rigours of modernity and present-day existence, thus preserving their rich cultural heritage in its pristine form. Things are however changing rapidly. Though there is mention of Donyi Polo (the Sun and Moon whom they worship as Gods), *apong*, *gale* (the cloth worn by the ladies in the lower portion of the body) and *galuk* (jacket worn by man), the Adi *apong*, the Khamti *lungi* (Dai, 2003: 1), the Buddhist tradition, butter tea (Dai, 2003: 20), *surpi* (a food item like butter), *ekung* and *onger* (Dai, 2003: 51), Solung Festival (Dai, 2003: 55), Ponung dance (Dai, 2003: 58), *mosup* (Dai, 2003: 75), the important issue that the writer is dealing with is the sudden and drastic changes taking place in the Arunachalee society. He is concerned with the thirst for money and power in man. However, Dai is primarily concerned with the growing threat of materialism that threatens to tear apart a society that for ages had greatly valued its community life.

Yeshe Dorjee Thongchi's published novels include *Sonam* (1981), *Lingjhik* (A Pillar, 1983), *Mouno Ounth Mukhar Hriday* (Silent Lips Murmuring Hearts, 2001), and *Sava Kota Manuh* (The Man Who Slices Dead Bodies, 2004). Most of the novels of Yeshe Dorjee Thongchi deal with the traditional and cultural life of the Monpa and the Sherdukpen tribes. The appeal of his novels lies in its being rooted in an indigenous tribe and its culture and at the same time bearing a pervading tone of universality.

His first published novel *Sonam* (1981) centres round the Brokpa tribe (a section of the Monpas). The family system of the Brokpas where a woman is socially allowed to marry more than one man is the custom around which the story of the novel revolves. In such a society, polygamy and polyandry are socially permissible, and the trauma, agony and the conflict of the characters can be traced to such a system due to which the universal man–woman relationship is affected. More importantly, being written for a people who do not belong to his native community, it is possible to look at the novel as an attempt on the part of the author to subvert the tendency of dominant societies to exoticize practices like polyandry. Further, it problematizes the outsider's common understanding of practices like polyandry by showing its contextual exigencies.

Lingjik (1983), the second novel by Yeshe Dorjee Thongchi, is basically about an old custom which was almost dead by the time in which the novel is set. But this old custom is given a fresh lease of life as a result of a clash between two persons leading to a clash between two clans. 'Lingjik' means 'a pillar of stone'. The Sherdukpens put the 'Lingjik' in the ground as the symbol of a very important decision or as the line of boundary to remind the heirs of the clan about that particular issue. They believe that if anyone violates that decision, the stone pillar would harm him/her. *Lingjik* is a novel where the author has talked about many rituals, customs and traditional beliefs which are not just commentaries on Arunachal Pradesh's tribal life but also help to carry forward the story.

In the Sahitya Akademi award-winning novel *Mouno Ounth Mukhar Hriday* (2001), Yeshe Dorjee Thongchi has adopted the universal theme of love which has been dealt in quite a different way. The story is set in the North East Frontier Agency (NEFA) of the 1950s. During the construction of a new road in one of the hilly areas of NEFA, two young people—a boy and a girl—belonging to different tribes fall for each other. The novel deals with the human feelings of love, hope, aspirations and dreams which transcend the limit of society and even that of language between two lovers.

Set against the background of the Monpa society of the 1950s and with references to different social, historical and political happenings of the time, Yeshe Dorjee Thongchi's *Sava Kota Manuh* is about a man whose profession is to slice dead bodies into pieces and his love for a saint. This novel centres round the Monpa custom of slicing dead bodies into one hundred and eight pieces.

Bishnu Rabha's novel *Mising Koneng* (Mising Girl) is based on the life of the Mising community of Assam. The novel was published in the second issue of the seventh year of *Amar Pratinidhi* (Our Representatives: Assamese periodical published from Calcutta). Later, it was included in *Bishnu Prasad Rabha Rachana Sambhar*, published by the Rabha Rachanawali Prakashan Sangha. The main focus of the novel is the love between Kumong and Parsoli. Both of them join the national freedom movement. The novel begins in a joyous moment of festive mood and celebration of the Mising community but ends in the disillusionment that follows the freedom. The ideals and philosophy of Rabha are well reflected in this novel. In this novel, Bishnu Rabha draws a picture of the assimilation of different ethnic and non-ethnic traditions and cultures. In this novel of Bishnu Rabha, the protagonist Kumong is a rebel who protests against the hatred and negligence meted out to the tribal people by the upper-caste Hindus. Kumong is not allowed to drink water from the same well that the upper-caste people use. He is not allowed to offer flowers to the idol of god in the temple. So he says, "Do not the Misings identify themselves as Assamese? In spite of being indigenous inhabitants of Assam, they do not qualify as Assamese unlike the Hindus!" (Rabha, 1989: 652). Perhaps this is the idea that Rabha wants to encourage. G. P. Sarma (2010) says,

> ...Besides being a piece of documentary literature and novel, it has got an additional richness to it. Because at the same time as it documents Mising society and its culture, this novel incorporates a discussion about building a healthy mutual relationship between the tribal people and the Assamese speaking people, and contains a healthy criticism of the attitude of the Assamese speaking people which stands in the way of building this relationship.

Rong Bong Terang illustrates the socio-cultural aspects of the Karbi society in his novel *Rongmilir Hanhi* (The Laughter of Rongmili, 1981). In *Rongmilir Hanhi*, a love story is presented against the backdrop of the social customs, rules and rituals of the Karbi people. Just like *Prithibir Hanhi*, *Rongmilir Hanhi* is also a social documentary. The beautiful unanimity and skilful handling of the complexity of human situations have prevented them from being mere documentaries. In *Rongmilir Hanhi*, Seng Teron is a youth who, being addicted to opium and suffering from tuberculosis, gradually inches closer to death. He is in love with Amphuk, Saraik's young daughter. This youth had once been a determined and strong character and had tried to rebuild his home after the death of his father. He had been told that only if he could give up his habit of taking opium, he would be able to win the hand of Amphuk and bring about improvement in his home. But since this does not happen, Saraik, her father, offers his daughter's hand to another youth from a different village. Even though following their social norms, the daughter bows down to her father's decisions, she is still in love with the sick young man. As she bids farewell to her first lover, she is rebuked by him and is called a cheat. But on hearing her rational explanation, he bids her farewell. It is not as if romantic love did not find a place in the Karbi hills in those days. But the youngsters were obligated to follow the social norms, and act rationally. There was physical attraction among the young men and women who came into contact through songs, dances and meetings; but physical attraction did not always bloom into romantic relationships.

There are a few Karbi writers who have contributed to Assamese literature through their novels. In most of their novels, the Karbi life and society is depicted with their customs and traditions. Karbi writers started writing fiction in the 1970s. Before that they had tried to document and translate the popular beliefs, myths and ballads which took the shape of a very rudimentary form of fictional writing. But these may not be called novels; instead it would be safer to assume that they laid the foundation for novel-writing amongst the Karbis.

Samsing Hanse's *Nam Tair Haimu* (Her Name is Haimu, 1974) can be called the first novel of this kind which is based on the Karbi *haimu* songs of tragic love involving the legendary lovers Long and Hai. In this story, we are introduced to the Karbi beliefs, the love and separation, pain and pleasure, and hopes and aspirations of the Karbi people. The *haimu* songs associated with the love story of Long and Hai are held in very high esteem by the Karbis. Samsing Hanse's *Nam Tair Haimu* deserves special mention not for the structure and technique of the novel but for depicting the honoured place that the *haimu songs* occupy in the minds of the Karbi people.

Jayanta Rongpi's novel *Puwate Ejak Dhanesh* (A Flight of Hornbills at Dawn) was published in 1977. In this novel, the Karbi social life is pictured. The colourful green hills and the daily lives of the Karbi people, their beliefs and rituals, and hopes and aspirations are depicted in the novel. The main focus of the novel is the material pressure from outside along with the cruel exploitation by the *mahajans* of the Karbi society. The novel talks about the class struggle of the deprived people. The novel might not be structurally perfect, but in the depiction of the Karbi society and the lives of the Karbi people and as a picture of the socio-economic conditions and problems of that ethnic group, *Puwate Ejak Dhanesh* deserves special mention.

Like the writers of Karbi community, writers from the Rabha community have also contributed to Assamese literature. Rajen Pam is a novelist from the Rabha community whose *Janong Jinong* (Live Life, 1990) presents a picture of the Rabhas and their lifestyles. The novel is full of traditional rites and rituals, folk beliefs, dresses and festivals of the Rabha society. In the Rabha society, there is a tradition of marrying the daughter of the maternal uncle. This traditional custom is not observed by the modern-day youths. The novel talks about a situation where going against the custom, a girl wants to avoid marrying her cousin. The girl named Juri commits suicide anticipating the pain of her separation from Jan. The novel, though small in size, depicts both the traditional Rabha society and the Rabha society in transition.

Khagen Rabha wrote another novel against the backdrop of the Rabha society. This novel called *Ramala* was published in 1997. The novel is not descriptive in nature. Though the novel does not refer to the problems confronting the Rabha community, there is an attempt to offer a journalistic account of the Rabha society. There might not be any in-depth probing into the character's minds, but the shattering of human values, traditional beliefs, age-old customs, and the resultant void and frustration form the core of the novel. Through the love story of Ramala and Kajak, the novelist tries to show how the age-old notion of unity and harmony is being threatened due to excessive consumption of local wine and also due to personal jealousy. The lovers are deeply in love with each other, but they remain separated due to the restrictive social customs and traditional beliefs. At the end, Kajak is portrayed as a frustrated character. Though the characters are not elaborately delineated, we have to cite this novel because of its attempt to picture the traditional Rabha society.

The Tradition of Assamese Ethnographic Novels 59

A few writers from the Mising community seem to take interest in portraying the Mising lives in their novels. The names worth mentioning in this regard are Tarun Chandra Pamegam, Bhaben Pegu, Ganesh Pegu, and Jatin Mipun. In their novels, we see a picture of the Mising community and the social life of the ethnic group which is depicted by the members of that community. All the three writers belong to that community.

Tarun Chandra Pamegam wrote two novels based on the lives of the Mising community. In his novel *Pahar Puri* (Hilly Place), he tries to draw the picture of the contemporary Mising society. At the same time, he imparts the rich fragrance and novelty of the hills and the life in the hills for the Misings. Though there is no direct reference to ethnic life and society in this novel, the mentality of the upper-caste Brahmins towards the tribes as well as the issues relating to inter-caste and inter-class issues are dealt with.

Pamegam's second novel *Xamajar Xesh Ximat* (At the Final Border of Society) is again set against the background of the Mising society. Like *Miri Jiyori*, the story of this novel revolves round the theme of love between Karmug and Oiseng. Of course, the novelist also introduces a host of other issues like addiction to opium, religion of the *ratikhowa* community, the impact of the Vaishnavite movement upon the Mising community. The reformist zeal in the novel seems to make it structurally weak and unattractive at times. In a very mild tone, the writer mentions the injustice meted out to the Mising people by the Hindu religious leaders.

Ganesh Pegu is another important Assamese novelist who belongs to the Mising community. His novel *Pahprir* (Butterfly) begged the best prize in the new writers' novel-writing competition in 1986. 'Pahprir' means butterfly. It is a novel based on the Mising social life. Here is a picture of the Mising society in transition. In this novel we see the protest against the exploitation of women in the name of tradition. The novelist tries to raise different issues related to the problems of the ethnic people and the lack of health care facility, education and transportation in the novel. The novelist tries to show how the ethnic society is neglected in every aspect of material and intellectual development. Due to the minute observation of the writer, the rites and rituals, customs and traditions, and the culture of the Mising community are very well expressed in the novel. This novel gives expression to the humanitarian philosophy of the writer.

Bhaben Pegu wrote two novels based on the ethnic community of the Misings. His first novel *Oiaow* (Beautiful) was published in 1987. The traditions and customs of the community with the description of various rituals, beliefs and superstitions, and ways of observing festivals are very well depicted in this novel. The writer talks about the slow pace of development and work ethics of the Mising people in this novel. In *Jiyadhalak Bhetiba Kone* (Who Will Embank the River Jiyadhal?), the river Jiyadhal is a living existence for the Mising community as a large section of this ethnic community lives beside the river.

Jatin Mipun wrote a novel called *Miksijili* (Stream of Teardrops) in 1993 against the backdrop of the Mising society. 'Miksijili' refers to drops of tear. The novel is about the powerful Baloram Yein who lives in Mahfala village. The picture of exploitation of the deprived by the powerful people is nicely depicted in this novel. The lifestyles and the beliefs and rituals of the community are also expressed in the novel. At last, Moneswari's son moves out to the town, thus leaving behind his mother who had looked after him with utmost care and difficulty. Mipun, the novelist, tries to delve deeper into the minds of his characters.

Though I have confined my discussion to ethnic novels written in Assamese in this chapter, it is obvious that even this apparently 'narrow' area suffices to provide a microcosm of the immensely rich and varied nature of this genre. Most of these fictions were written with the obvious and stated intention of holding up to its readers a 'true image' of ethnic lives and societies. It is also evident that Assamese ethnic fiction writers have generally tended to focus more on representing the beliefs and customs of ethnic communities instead of exploring the complex and intricate web of exploitation that has relegated them to the periphery. Does the North East feel excluded from the 'mainstream' of Indian culture and tradition? A cursory survey of the recent socio-political scenario of Assam seems to suggest that the answer to this question would be in the affirmative. Moreover, India's colonial inheritance is complicated by the multiethnic patterns of the inhabitants of North East India. While the Assamese in particular and the North East Indians in general, do have a sense of allegiance to racial and cultural origins outside this cartographic space, they also have a strong sense of marginality in relation to those other cultures from the 'mainstream' with which they are yet to be fully integrated.

The clamour for creation of new states and autonomous councils in North East India continue despite the creation of several new states and territorially defined autonomous councils for different tribes. This is not surprising because it is believed that an adequate share of political power is a necessary condition for retaining one's socio-cultural identity and development. Identity, perceived as being under threat, can only be 'protected' by inhabiting exclusive spaces and by securing a greater number for the group. Such cultural and developmental aspirations, though legitimate, face rough weather once they become connected with exclusive administrative boundaries for self-governance. Thus, community conflicts over land and territoriality continue to turn North East India into an area of unrest and crisis. As Sanjib Baruah (2008: 15–16) comments,

> This notion of ethnicity and the fixing of ethnic groups to particular physical spaces made it necessary to distinguish between so-called pure and impure types to account for those that strayed away from the assigned physical spaces, i e, living in the hills instead of the plains or vice versa, or living in the "wrong" hills; or those that did not conform to the ethnic stereotypes that colonial officials had about them.

As against this, some of the writers whom we have discussed here seem to continue to cling on to the image of a greater Assam that was championed by such icons of Assam's cultural life such as Bishnu Rabha and Bhupen Hazarika. This seems to be particularly true in the case of writers who started writing within three decades of India's independence. There was a lot of hope and optimism about the future of the nation as reflected in the fiction of Lummer Dai. The difference in perspective of the relatively younger generation of writers is perceivable when one compares the fiction of Lummer Dai with that of Yeshe Dorjee Thongchi; as against Dai's hope and optimism about the success of the nation-state (to some extent this optimism is subjected to a closer scrutiny in his last novel *Upar Mahal*), Thongchi problematizes the conventional understanding of development. In fact, many contemporary writers from around the country have critiqued the model of development that was adopted both by the colonial masters and their Indian counterparts after the independence of the country.

Problematizing the Identity of the Author as Cultural Insider

Following poststructuralism, it is no longer unproblematic to categorize a writer as 'ethnic' or 'non-ethnic' and it is equally difficult to call an author as a cultural insider or outsider. Generally, if a writer writes about the community he/she belongs to, he/she is considered as an insider of that community. However, it is important to keep in mind that the author's identity is in a state of constant flux. Even if we do not go to the extent of declaring the "death of the author" like Roland Barthes (2001: 1469), we can no longer be unmindful of the fact that the text is a "tissue of quotations" born out of *a priori* knowledge.

In this section, I will make an analysis of two novels which have portrayed the lives and societies of two ethnic communities of North East India. Both the novels depict the rites and rituals, the lifestyles of the ethnic communities that the novels are set against. Yeshe Dorjee Thongchi, the author of the novel *Mouno Ounth Mukhar Hriday* (Silent Lips, Murmuring Hearts) 'belongs to' the community about which he is writing, while Rasna Baruah (Birinchi Kumar Baruah) writes about the tea-garden community (a community that he does not 'belong to') of an imagined tea garden of Assam in his novel *Seuji Patar Kahini*. It is accepted that *Seuji Patar Kahini* deals with many issues related to the complexities of human life and relationships rather than being a mere depiction of the tea-garden community with its culture and tradition. Thongchi's *Mouno Ounth Mukhar Hriday* too introduces various issues of love and of human relationships in the course of the novel. Rasna Baruah writes about a community which is outside his own, while Thongchi writes about the community of Arunachal Pradesh which he belongs to. As such, Baruah is an outsider while Thongchi is a cultural insider in his fiction.

Rasna Baruah depicts the life in the tea gardens of Assam in his novel *Seuji Patar Kahini* (published in 1959). Baruah, though a cultural outsider, is very much involved with the society and the emotions of each and every characters of the novel. It is difficult to label him as an outsider when we analyse this ethnic novel. Neither can we consider him as someone who is a distant observer of the community he is presenting. He is in no way a 'charmed' spectator of the community he is writing about. In spite of being a cultural 'outsider' to the adivasi tribe, Baruah is not "a careful but distant observer, a charmed spectator of the tribal society" (Sarma, 2010), but he is one who is passionately involved with the lives and characters of his novel. While presenting different aspects of the lives of the ethnic community of the tea garden, the novelist tries to overcome the tendency of non-ethnic writers to look at ethnic communities from an outsider's perspective or from the position of someone belonging to more 'developed' societies. Though a 'cultural outsider', Baruah locates himself within the community through his depiction of the characters and events of the novel.

I wish to focus my discussion on the issue of authorship (cultural identity of the authors) of these novels. The novel *Mouno Ounth Mukhar Hriday* is written by an 'insider' (member of that particular community) but the novel *Seuji Patar Kahini* is written by an 'outsider' (member outside that community). Just as Baruah being a cultural outsider is passionately involved with the characters of his novel, Yeshe Dorjee Thongchi, though an 'insider', appears to be more a detached observer in some ways. He is someone who can objectively look at the society he presents even though he belongs to that society. In fact, he is shuffling between the identities of one who is culturally very close to his own society and someone who is emotionally detached from the society to which he belongs. I shall focus on the problems arising out of reading too much into the category of insider/outsider in case of a creative writer. In analyzing the novels, I would also like to bring up the issue of 'shifting identities'.

Though written about the 'universal' theme of love, Thongchi portrays the ethnic societies of Arunachal Pradesh, particularly the customs and traditions, rituals and beliefs of the Nyishi and Sherdukpen community in his novel *Mouno Ounth Mukhar Hriday*. And I believe that the author's 'shifting identities' is at the root in rendering a multilayered meaning to it. Thongchi is a part of the community when he is a true admirer of the age-old traditions and beliefs of his ethnic community. Moreover, when he dreams of the development of the state with its educational institutions, hospitals and industries that would crop up and be managed and run by the people from the state, Thongchi is an 'insider' of the community he is writing about:

> A day would come when this land of NEFA could be considered a developed place. There would be schools, colleges, hospitals and industries in these hills and the local people would run these as teachers, doctors, engineers and industrialists. The day when the light of education would illuminate these hills was not very far off. (Thongchi, 2010: 132)

In describing the eternal human feelings, in the expression of love and hatred, pain and pleasure, Thongchi's identity is not merely restricted to that of a member of an ethnic community. In fact, at times he seems to be an outsider of the community that he belongs to.

Dilip Saikia is a character of the novel through which the writer expresses his beliefs, hopes and aspirations. It is interesting to note that while expressing his views through Dilip Saikia (a member outside the ethnic group), Thongchi plays the role of an outsider. Dilip Saikia, the field assistant responsible for the construction of the road, takes particular care to bring the ethnic communities together. It is obvious that his mission is not merely the construction of the road, but to build bridges across the diverse ethnic groups so that all their misgivings regarding one another are done away with.

The multilayered identity of the author in Thongchi is discernible on many occasions in the novel. He deliberately shuffles between the position of an insider and that of an outsider in *Mouno Ounth Mukhar Hriday*. While most of the time he appears to be an insider with a deep sense of affiliation with the Arunachalee society, occasionally he appears as a detached observer. We see the writer adopting the latter perspective when he tries to appreciate a haunting melody of a song sung by a girl from the Nyishi camp through the words of Dilip Saikia:

> Even though he could not understand the language, he felt the lilting song have a sort of magical effect. It held the same kind of appeal as the body of an unknown girl of an unknown tribe. (Thongchi, 2010: 18)

It is important to mention here that the concept of ethnic identity formation is itself not distinct. The process of identity formation in an ethnic community is dependent on various other factors. It is related to time, place, education, population, political power, etc. All these factors directly or indirectly influence the process of identity formation of an individual or of a society. I would like to cite an example from Arunachal Pradesh. Within the state an individual from a particular ethnic community would like to be introduced as a member of that particular community, but outside the state he/she would like to be introduced as a member of an ethnic community of Arunachal Pradesh rather than as an Adi, Sherdukpen, Nyishi, Apatani, Khamti, Galo. Wangcho, etc. At the time of his/her speech about the ethnic groups of Arunachal, one from any ethnic group of Arunachal Pradesh may like to be introduced as a member of an ethnic group of Arunachal. But while the same person (suppose from the Sherdukpen community) would like to say something about any other ethnic community of his state, he/she adopts a different point of view. Thongchi literally plays with this sense of dual identity in his novel from time to time. And I believe in the analysis of the novel *Mouno Ounth Mukhar Hriday*, the author's multiple identities and his position both as a member of Arunachalee society in general and as a member of the Sherdukpen community in particular need to be looked at. Consciously, Yeshe Dorjee Thongchi is an Arunachalee. He is not happy with the singular identity of a Sherdukpen, nor does he want to be introduced only as a Sherdukpen. He is an Arunachalee first and as an Arunachalee he dreams to bring unity and fellow feeling among the members of the different ethnic communities of the state.

Towards the end of the novel we see the expression of such conscious thoughts of the author. At last all the characters of the novel come to realize that all human beings are the same; he advocates the same human values, love and friendship, pain and pleasures for the whole state. The conversation of Yama's brother Tadak and Rinchin reflects such ideas clearly:

> We Bhutias think that we are the greatest race while you Nyshis think that you are the greatest. That is why we hate each other. We consider each other our enemies and fight. But having stayed with you during the construction

of the road I have come to know that we are the same. It is just that we speak different languages, follow different customs, and wear different clothes but our minds are the same. (Thongchi, 2010: 123)

Though consciously Thongchi is a member of Arunachalee society at large, sometimes his identity as a Sherdukpen manages to sneak through. This is why Thongchi stresses upon the patience and perseverance of the Sherdukpen community (Thongchi, 2010: 12) and also on the worship of God through lighting *diya* (earthen lamps) with ghee except instead of offering blood to the deity (Thongchi, 2010: 56). When Rinchin says that they do not follow the custom of offering blood to the deity, we discern a sense of superiority. Interestingly, Thongchi is also a Sherdukpen. The similar feeling of supremacy is discernible in the description of the Sherdukpen dance forms like Yak dance, Ajyi Lamu dance and Tsange dances as 'richer' than the Nyishi dance forms. Looking at the Sherdukpens performing in front of the governor of Assam at Tanga of Kameng district, Yama and Yado start to think:

It seemed to the Nyishi girls that in comparison to the Sherdukpens, their own dances were quite ordinary. (Thongchi, 2010: 171)

In the unconscious mind though he seems to be more attached to his community and to love and respect his own rituals, customs and traditions more than anything else, his conscious self always strives for the upliftment of the Arunachalee society. In the actual self he is a true lover of his state. On several occasions, Thongchi expresses his own views through the character of Dilip Saikia who is an Assamese youth working in Arunachal Pradesh. It is important to note that Dilip Saikia is respectful of the Arunachalee society and its people. He is also concerned with the pains and problems, and hopes and aspirations of the people of the state. Here the author takes the position of an outsider in the portrayal of the life and society of Arunachal Pradesh. He might also be assuming the role of a non-Arunachalee to maintain emotional detachment.

In the novel *Seuji Patar Kahini*, the author depicts three different societies: the colonial English society sheltered in the tea gardens of Assam, the village life of Assam with decayed heritage, and the adivasi society in the same tea gardens of the state. And in depicting these three different societies, the author appears to be an insider to the adivasi community of the imaginary tea garden of Assam. Rasna Baruah is able to adopt an emic perspective to depict the pains and sufferings of the adivasi community. He talks about the exploitation of the tea gardeners by the British colonial officers. He is conscious about the complexities of human relationship, human nature and human feelings. Therefore, we see him equally at ease in drawing the characters of Sonia and Nareswar. Nareswar is an Assamese youth from a village who is in love with Sonia as well as the tea-garden life around him. But he could not permanently settle in the garden. Neither could he marry Sonia. On the other hand, Sonia, born in a tea-garden community, does not however feel attached to it, nor does she enjoy the life in the garden. In fact, on several occasions she criticizes the lifestyles, rituals and customs of the adivasi society.

What is significant here is the fact that in *Seuji Patar Kahini*, it is not only the author but the main characters of the novel too who deliberately shuffle between the concept of insider and outsider. The main character Sonia is born out of the union of an adivasi mother and a British officer father. Therefore, her identity is characterized by an 'in-between-ness'. She describes that it is her white skin that separates her from her companions. She could never belong to her father's society because she is not recognized by her father. In her own words she is "born out of the attack of a beastly *sahib* on her mother" (Barua, 1997: 149). Therefore, her biological father is not her legal father. On the other hand, though born to an adivasi mother, she does not feel attached to the tea garden. Sonia is a character which speaks against the economic, social and even physical exploitation of the tea-garden people by the *sahibs*. Sonia is not ready to accept everything simply and unquestioningly in the name of tradition. She prefers to live her life according to her likes and dislikes.

Hiren Gohain sees the novel *Seuji Patar Kahini* as a search for a more beautiful attitude towards life than that offered by the natural and traditional lifestyles of human beings (Preface to *Seuji Patar Kahini*). According to Gohain, the quest for something new and beautiful remains unfulfilled till the end of the novel. And it is this unfulfilled desire, this quest which the author attempts to represent through the character of Nareswar.

The author is conscious of the plight of the tea gardeners and the cruel, inhuman torture that they have to suffer due to the prevalent social system. The omniscient narrator seems to be more sympathetic to the voice of protest. And this voice is of Sonia who revolts fearlessly against the inhuman torture meted out to the tea-garden labourers by the British officers. In fact, Sonia is critical of the religious teachings of the Christian priests who keep on advising people to accept this exploitation saying that if someone slaps you on your right cheek, let him do that on the left cheek too. She says that even after witnessing the terrible sufferings and inhuman punishment of the *coolies*, the priests never stop advising people to accept the punishment. While describing the condition of the tea-garden people, the punishment that they have to suffer due to simple mistakes, the author takes the position of an insider who can identify with the people. While he is also sympathetic to the character of Sonia who is depicted as a strong female character, the author is actually critical of the prevalent social system.

All said and done, there is a striking difference between the two novels under discussion. Rasna Barua's novel is about political correctness and about a worldview which might be said to be fundamentally alien to the adivasis. Thongchi's novel is politically more interesting as a representation of ethnic life in the sense that it looks at the ways in which an ethnic group constructs itself and its other. Thongchi's novel reflects the idioms of resistance offered by the 'indigenous' ethnic groups which reflect the general sense of fear amongst the indigenous ethnic communities of North East India of getting marginalized in the face of massive immigration. There is a strong sense of indigeneity that runs through Thongchi's novel; the fear of outsiders grabbing hold of the land and resources of an indigenous ethnic group is manifested in Thongchi's novel. However, as we shall see in the next chapter, writers like Mahasweta Devi problematize an easy understanding of the writer as a cultural 'insider' or 'outsider'.

3
Forests, Human Rights and Development: A Cross-Cultural Study of Select Novels of Yeshe Dorjee Thongchi, Pratibha Ray and Mahasweta Devi

Let me start this chapter with a reference to Jawaharlal Nehru's foreword to the first edition of Verrier Elwin's *A Philosophy for NEFA*. Nehru, in this foreword, expresses his dilemma regarding the tribes of Arunachal Pradesh (then North-East Frontier Agency [NEFA]). Nehru wonders if it would be good to let the preliterate tribes to live in their own, original set-up or to make them aware of the culture and tradition of the outside world:

> It was true that they [the people of Arunachal] could not be left cut off from the world as they were. Political and economic forces impinged upon them and it was not possible or desirable to isolate them. Equally undesirable it seemed to me, was to allow these forces to function freely and upset their whole life and culture, which had so much of good in them. (Elwin, 1959: Foreword)

In many ways, Nehru's views, though stated very briefly, hints at the concerns that we frequently come across in critiques of development that have emerged in diverse fields in recent times. Obviously, contemporary thinkers would probably say that Nehru's views reveal a bias in favour of a universally acceptable model of development. I have reservations about Nehru's statements on two fronts: on the one hand, in spite of his professed belief, it cannot be denied that Nehru romanticises the idea of preservation of the idyllic way of life of the tribes; secondly, he does not seem to consider the possibility of having a more flexible and inclusive notion of development.

Opinions have been sharply divided in so far as the Nehru–Elwinian policy towards the tribes of the North East is concerned. Srikanth and Thomas (2005: 57), for instance, adopt a highly critical stance:

> As a part of its nation-building effort, the post-colonial Indian state sought to integrate ... in the so-called 'excluded' and 'partially excluded' areas of British India into the Indian Union. Through a carrot and stick policy, the Indian state tried to ensure that majority of indigenous ethnic communities living in the Northeast join the Indian federation.

Some others have tended to be a lot more sympathetic in their views. The Nehruvian path to nation-building was paved with "good intentions" and aimed to give rise to the cultural politics of representation through the creation of a separate space for the re-articulation of the native communities within the nationalist discourse (Biswas and Suklabaidya, 2008: 110).

Michael Cowen and Robert Shenton (1995: 27) have remarked that 'development' is one of "the central organizing concepts of our time". In this context, it is particularly interesting to look at the ways in which issues of development, man–environment relationship and rights of indigenous communities are addressed in contemporary Indian literature. The forest, either as a metaphorical space for projecting one's fears or as a living reality that shapes the lives of communities living in and around it, has found frequent mention in classical texts of Indian literature including the epics.

In the Indian context, 'forest' and 'development' have a deep-seated connection; to put it more clearly, forest was seen for a long time as a symbol of all that was antithetical to the idea of development. The first step towards development, it was thought, was to clear the forests and to 'civilize' the people who lived in it. Wherever the rhetoric of development has found acceptance in India, it has paved the way for civilizing missions that have strived to impose the way of life of one group of people over another. In the Indian context, it is also very important to be appreciative of the very different relationship between man and environment, and thus, by extension, between man and forest. In India, forest is not external to the lives of the people. It is, in fact, a site of struggle; it is a matter of survival for the people whose daily bread depends upon it. Thus, our whole approach to development needs to be radically altered, or even completely inverted to facilitate any attempt to bring about positive changes in the way of life of the people. In other words, when we talk about development of the ethnic people we should look at it from their perspective. As argued earlier, so long as we overcome the urge to remain obsessed with a universally workable model of development, we can see that ideas of development should be understood in terms of the aspirations of the community for whom that development is apparently made. G.N. Devy (2011: 133) says, "Development is a ceaseless process ... the beginning of development comes from the definite urge for bringing about a change in a person, family and the society."

In this study, I will look at the ways in which Yeshe Dorjee Thongchi, Pratibha Ray and Mahasweta Devi address issues of development and human rights of indigenous communities in their fiction. I will focus attention on Thongchi's *Mouno Ounth Mukhar Hriday* (Silent Lips Murmuring Hearts), Pratibha Ray's *Adibhumi* (The Primal Land) and Mahasweta Devi's *Aranyer Adhikar* (Right over the Forest).

An inhabitant belonging to a tribe in the region of Singhbhum, near the border of the states of West Bengal and Bihar, once said to Mahasweta Devi, "When these forests disappear, we will also disappear" (Wenzel, 1988: 127). Forest is the source of survival for majority of the ethnic communities of India. In the paper mentioned above, Jennifer Wenzel mentions Vandana Shiva who is a philosopher, an environmental activist and an eco-feminist. She plays a major role in the global eco-feminist movement. Shiva participated in the Chipko movement in the 1970s.

Mentioning Vandana Shiva, Jennifer Wenzel (1988: 130) says that there is no doubt that India "is a forest culture, but it is a culture that has been defined, throughout its long history, as much by contests over its forests as by peaceful existence within them". Citing the reference of Rig Veda in her book *Ecology and the Politics of Survival: Conflicts over Natural Resources in India* (1991: 75), Shiva describes the forests as "Aranyani or mother Goddess who takes care of wildlife and ensures the availability of food to man". Shiva (1991: 32) terms Western environmentalism as "luxury of the rich" and contrasts it with Third World Movements that are "a survival imperative for majority of people whose survival is not taken care of by the market economy but is threatened by its expansion".

According to Vandana Shiva, the way these development paradigms are being implemented—through violence against nature and women—threatens survival itself. In her book *Staying Alive: Women, Ecology and Survival in India* (1988), Shiva focuses on how rural Indian women experience and perceive the causes and effects of ecological destruction. The application of a readymade framework imported from the West as a model for development in India is fraught with dangers. Shiva's critiques of development and of the European model of enlightenment stem from the belief that the people who live in the land should have a greater say in deciding the mandate of development. In this seminal work, she connects development with colonialism and the oppression of women. Her argument, backed up with sufficient facts and figures, is persuasive and moving, thus challenging readers to rethink development in the global South.

In an interview with Wilma Massucco, Vandana Shiva (2007) says that it is important to see the earth as a mother. She has given three reasons in support of her argument and the first point says that:

> Most of the time, when we think of the Earth as dead and inert and just as a source of raw materials, we create illusions that money and welfare come from Wall Street and factories. We forget that for every factory the first material is contributed by the earth. (Shiva, 2007)

In the same interview, Shiva (2007) expresses her views about development in the following words:

> My concept of development is that it must be defined by the people for whom it is supposed to be, it cannot be defined by Washington or by the politicians. It has to be defined by the community, and if the community feels that letting the river flow is development, then they let the river flow. If the community feels building a dam is good then they can build a dam, but it shouldn't be that they are told you have no rights to decide.

Ethnocritics have talked about the harmony between man and nature. Ethnocriticism believes that issues relating to a society should be analysed from within that society's perspective. G.N. Devy (2011: 126) says, "The modern discourse on development has come to India from the West ... this concept is dominated by the widely prevalent technological and industrial culture."

Yeshe Dorjee Thongchi is one of the most familiar names for the contemporary readers of Assamese literature. In a world abounding with clichéd stories of sleaze, terrorism and the decadence of city life, Thongchi's work comes as a breath of fresh air. A Sherdukpen, Thongchi generally portrays the societies of the Sherdukpens and Monpas living in the frontier areas of Arunachal Pradesh, especially of Dirang and Tawang. The novel *Mouno Ounth Mukhar Hriday* is a tragic love story set against the backdrop of Arunachal Pradesh going through a process of rapid transition in the 1950s. The novel has been translated into English as *Silent Lips Murmuring Hearts*. Rinchin and Yama are two unlucky lovers from two different tribes (Sherdukpen and Nyishi, respectively) who meet in the Chaku hills during the construction of a road where they serve as voluntary workers. The road is a metaphorical representation of development. Initially the tribes view each other with suspicion, but when the time comes to part, they do so with heavy hearts. Dilip Saikia, the field assistant responsible for the construction of the road, takes particular care to bring the tribes together. It is obvious that his mission is not merely the construction of the road, but to build bridges across the diverse tribes so that all their misgivings regarding one another are done away with. Under the loving and able guidance of Dilip Saikia, the Nyishis and Sherdukpens come together to work as a team. The story of Rinchin and Yama ends on a tragic note but Dilip Saikia's dream of bringing together the tribes materializes as they come to respect each other's differences. The world of *Mouno Ounth Mukhar Hriday* is multilingual and multiethnic and nation-building appears to be one of the crucial themes of the novel.

Nation-building refers to the process of structuring a nation using the power of the state. This process aims at the unification of the people or peoples within the state so that it remains politically stable and viable in the long run. A nation builds itself with the help of the symbolic structures such as schools, hospitals, industries, and so on. Benedict Anderson's concept of the nation as an 'imagined geography' or as an 'imagined community' would be an appropriate tool to show how the nation is a community socially constructed and ultimately imagined by the people who perceive themselves as part of that group as in *Mouno Ounth Mukhar Hriday*. Benedict Anderson (2006: 6) defined a nation as "an imagined political community [that is] imagined as both inherently limited and sovereign". An imagined community is different from an actual community because it is not (and cannot be) based on quotidian face-to-face interaction between its members. Instead, members hold in their minds a mental image of their affinity. As Anderson (2006: 6) puts it, a nation "is imagined because the members of even the smallest nation will never know most of their fellow-members, meet them, or even hear of them, yet in the minds of each lives the image of their communion".

In the 1950s, Arunachal Pradesh was known as the North-East Frontier Agency (NEFA). During the British rule, no serious efforts were made to put an administrative system into operation in this hilly terrain. It was only after independence that the Indian Government took steps to provide a sound administrative infrastructure in this land which was quite 'backward'. As a result, the district headquarters established during the British regime had to be shifted from the present-day Assam to Bomdila, Ziro, Tezu and Khonsa. Plans were going on for the construction of roads so as to connect these headquarters to the plains. But it was a difficult task to find labourers willing to go to the NEFA of those days. So the local population was engaged for the work. One member from every family of each village had to devote himself to the construction of the road. The process of linking Bomdila, headquarter of the Kameng frontier division, started from Missamari. By 1968, a road was constructed till Chaku. Work on the remaining portion of the road from Chaku to Bomdila was begun in autumn. Dilip Saikia was given the task of constructing an extremely difficult portion of the road.

When the Nyishis and Sherdukpens meet for the first time in the Chaku hills, the hearts of many of the members of Rinchin's group pound with fear because they had heard many stories about the Nyishis since their childhood. They had heard mainly about the aggressive nature of the Nyishis, and so they were scared that the Nyishis would turn violent and hack them to pieces. Hesitatingly, the group moved inside the Nyishi camp, placing their trust in Dilip Saikia, Rinchin Norbu and a few bold male members. When the Sherdukpens refuse to stay in a camp near the Nyishis, Dilip Saikia is reminded that just before they had started construction of the road, the *Bada* Sahib had invited all the employees for a feast at his place. In his speech the *Bada* Sahib had said:

> Our mission is not merely to build a road through the hills; we should also work towards making our way through the mental barrier of the hill tribes. Different tribes even when staying on the same hill do not recognize each other. And even if they do, they look at each other suspiciously owing to their long-standing rivalry. They do not want to mingle with others; they do not want to live together or work together. During the process of road construction, we will make the different tribes stay together to rid them of their misgivings about each other. We must bring them together and cement a bond of trust between them. (Thongchi, 2010: 37)

Trying to convince Rinchin and his group of the need to stay together, Dilip Saikia repeats the words of the *Bada* Sahib:

> Tell your people that the government has ordered them to cooperate with the Nyishis. Along with the construction of the road, we should strive to bring unity and harmony amongst the different tribes and the inhabitants of different villages by removing all their misgivings. That is the reason for asking you to stay along with the Nyishis and work with them. (Thongchi, 2010: 38)

He goes on to say,

> The road that we will build together will not only connect the hills with the plains, but will also foster unity amongst your tribes and make a composite race out of you all. I know that even though you all live in the hills, you are not familiar with one another. Once the road comes up, you will get a lot of opportunities to visit each other's places and to trade. (Thongchi, 2010: 38)

The modern nation was created by the unification of various groups of people into a common society or community, which takes the 19th century nation-state form, forged out of disciplinary institutions such as the school, the army or the factory. National identity needs to be deliberately constructed by moulding different groups into a nation. Nation-building can involve the use of propaganda or major infrastructure development to foster social harmony and economic growth. After Tadak and Rinchin had interpreted his words in their own languages, Dilip Saikia speaks again to the voluntary workers:

> Once you complete the construction of the road, Bomdila will be connected to towns like Tezpur, Guwahati and Shillong. The hills and plains will come closer. Motor vehicles will ply on this road…. Once the roads are built, the hills will develop like the plains. There will be schools, hospitals, tin-roofed houses, shops and markets. So everyone must cooperate to finish the construction of the road within a short spell of time. (Thongchi, 2010: 51)

While highlighting the process of nation-building, Thongchi also expresses his apprehensions about the drastic changes that the process of development would bring about:

> [NEFA] was a place untouched by modern civilization and its forests and rivers possessed a virgin glory. Though the tribes survived essentially on fish and meat they obtained from the rivers and forests, they had also attended to their conservation…. But of late, the so-called process of development has affected the forests and the rivers. The use of gun in place of bows and arrows, chemical drugs and dynamites for killing fish instead of resorting to traditional methods had led to the wiping out of the animals, birds and fish. (Thongchi, 2010: 66)

Among the contemporary female fiction writers of Orissa, Pratibha Ray would undoubtedly rank as one of the most accomplished. With an impressive corpus of eighteen novels, seventeen collections of short stories, one travelogue, and nine books for children and ten for neo-literates, she has received numerous awards including the Sarala Award and the Orissa Sahitya Akademi award, the latter for her novel *Shilapadma* (Stone Lotus) in 1985. She received the Moorti Devi Award in 1991 for her widely acclaimed novel *Yagnaseni* (Draupadi). A former professor of Education, she was a member of the Orissa Public Service Commission. Ray's fictional world is not an imaginary landscape. It is rooted in a concrete socio-historical context and in Orissa's cultural heritage. Prafulla Kumar Mohanty (2013: 38) remarks that Ray's range is "vast and varied" and her narratives too are "expressive, interpretive, argumentative and at times even magical". Ray "takes these little known figures to the larger scene of India's struggle for freedom and makes them heroic, sacrificial and grand. She however does not call her work 'history'; she fictionalizes facts without the dispassionateness of a historian" (Mohanty, 2013: 38).

Her novel *Adibhumi*, published in a translation as *The Primal Land* by Orient Longman in 2001, involves the changes in the social and cultural life of the Bondas. Her research on the lifestyle and behaviour of Bondo highlanders took her to the remote hills of the Koraput district of Orissa. An intimate study of Bondo life finds expression in her novel *Adibhumi*. This classic work is a meticulously researched fictional reconstruction of the life of the Bonda tribe. It is a novelized ethnography of the Bonda people, a tribe living deep in the forested plateau of the remote Malkangiri district on Orissa's south western tips, where Ray carried out her research as an anthopology student in the 1970s.

Adibhumi was published in 1993. However, the novel ran into rough weather in 2004 when members of some tribes strongly reacted to the depiction of a sexual relationship between father-in-law and daughter-in-law in the Bonda community. Ray's literary world depicts the marriage of mature girls of 18–20 of age to tender boys who are 10–12 years old. As expected, the child-groom in such cases is very often supposed to be taken care of like a mother by the bride. Sometimes, taking this opportunity, the father-in-law develops a sexual relationship with his son's wife. This is an event that is narrated as one of the stories in the novel. Some have alleged that Pratibha Ray, the writer of *Adibhumi*, has done serious damage to the moral ethics of the community. In any case, fictional reality is not to be seen as a lived reality.

It is important to note that in anthropology, the sexual life and sexual behaviour of many tribes are described vividly to maintain the truth, so the grounds on which Ray has been criticized hardly carry much weight as she is a creative writer and therefore, enjoys a greater degree of freedom than other fields would permit. Secondly, if we accept that the creative writer has to maintain the 'purity' of cultural representation, she might definitely have to deal with contentious issues related to a tribe. While writing fiction based on any ethnic group, the writer can combine his or her own imagination with historical facts, but obviously there should not be any distortion of facts. As has already been said, *Adibhumi* is a meticulously researched fictional reconstruction of the life of the Bonda tribe, and the readers are introduced to the lives and the different cultural traditions of this tribe in this novel.

> The Bondunis searched the jungle for roots, leaves, mushrooms and insects to eat. (Ray, 2001: 224)

Forest plays a very important role in the lives of the ethnic people not only "because the tribals have sustained themselves on forest as a resource of their livlihood" (Sen and Yadav, 2008: 27) but also for their close association with Nature at large. In *Adibhumi*, this close attachment of the Bonda tribe with the forest is well represented:

> There was no lack of virgin forest; the land was free to everyone who needed it.... The mountains teemed with salap trees, birds and beasts, worms and insects: no Bonda went hungry ... now the naked jungle bared its teeth at the Bonda to taunt him: "You have been cutting down my trees; now you must pay the price. The birds and beasts, the fruits and roots, the rain and the wind will all disappear, and you will burn in the scorching sun." (Ray, 2001: 65)

And

> The Bonda owns everything here—the clouds, the sky, the mountains, forests, waterfalls, the terraced fields, trees, animals. Hemmed in and guarded by the life and death. (Ray, 2001: 2)

This is also true of the other tribes. The tea-garden labourers' association with the tea plants and the dependence of their lives on the tea plants are appropriately depicted in the Assamese novel *Seuji Patar Kahini* by Rasna Barua.

> We grow in the midst of the tea garden breastfed by our mothers and frolicing around in the midst of tea plants.... A mother looks after her child, but we take care of the tea plants till they mature.... Tea plants keep us young. (Barua, 1997: 108; my translation)

In the same novel, Rasna Barua talks about the deep attachment between a coolie and the tea plants. This deep sense of attachment is reflected in a sentence uttered by Sonia:

> The coolie can part from his parents, his spouse and even his children- but he cannot part with the tea-plants. (Barua, 1997: 131; my translation)

The Bonda's beliefs and rituals are connected to Nature. They consider Nature as an integral part of their daily life and ways of worship. For them, God manifests Himself in different forms and shapes.

> The gods and goddesses whom the Bonda worship do not need stone images carved by man: they manifest themselves to him in different forms, as they please—a rock, a tree, a lake, a tiger, a ghost. (Ray, 2001: 199)

All of them are so attached to forests, rivers and mountains, and, in general, to Nature at large that it is very difficult to talk about them as distinct from Nature. It is seen in *Adibhumi* that different developmental projects are taken up by the government in the interior areas of the Bonda mountain which is completely secluded from the outside world. While these projects are claimed to be undertaken for the welfare of the tribes of the Koraput hills, those people are being, in fact, detached from their roots, from the age-old beliefs and from their traditional rituals in the name of development. As a result of these development projects, many people of the Bonda community consciously or unconsciously have started to detach themselves from the forest or the forest economy. Arundhati Roy (2011: 1) has written about the impact of 'development' on the Kondh tribe of Orissa:

> The low, flat-topped hills of south Orissa have been home to the Dongria Kondh long before there was a country called India or a state called Orissa. The hills watched over the Kondh. The Kondh watched over the hills and worshipped them as living deities. Now these hills have been sold for the bauxite they contain. For the Kondh it's as though god has been sold.

The story of the Bonda in *Adibhumi* parallels the various government attempts at development and 'civilizing' the tribes, and this has both comic and, at times, devastatingly tragic results. In this 'civilizing' process of the Bonda people, the government officials very often display an insensitivity to the issues of human rights. Besides, on many occasions, it is clearly shown in the novel that the ethnic people are exploited by the so-called 'civilized' people of the plains. In the name of imparting education among the tribes of this mountain, the government sets up a few schools in the remote hilly regions of Koraput. Significantly, these schools are functioning only on pen and paper. In reality, there is not a single school running. The conversation between Sitanath Sahu (who visits the Khairput hill on a project) and Mohan Babu (the school teacher) very clearly reflects this situation. Mohan Babu's explanation of the "brilliant functioning" of schools where there are no teachers and no students (Ray, 2001: 130) is understandable only when he answers Sitanath Sahu's question: "Then how do all these schools function?" He answers Sitanath Sahu by saying: "Perfectly, sir. But only on paper.... The teachers can't come up to the schools, so the schools come down to the teachers"(Ray, 2001: 131).

Moreover, in other developmental projects too, the government officials exploit the mountain dwellers just because they cannot understand the language of the officers, and the officers too are unable to communicate with them. The interpreter exploits the situation to his benefit. It is mentioned in the novel that the students belonging to tribes were given onions and watery rice to eat, but when officials from the Welfare Department visited the school to make enquiries, the students reported that they had had meat, fish, *daal* and vegetables (Ray, 2001: 232). The students of the schools were engaged in many household activities like washing utensils, clothes and even cleaning the lavatories of their teachers.

The government contractors try their best to acquire more and more money or wealth by working for the ethnic people of the hills. The writer illustrates this aspect by stating that the wages paid to each Bonduni was much lesser than the prescribed rates of the government. But the contractor complains that he has been forced to pay each female coolie twice the approved wage. The government reimburses the contractor; the money sanctioned for the construction of the road runs out and the work remains incomplete (Ray, 2001: 222). The Education Department is concerned more with the number of students who passed, not the depth of their learning (Ray, 2001: 233). This is the reason why the records of the number of students who passed the exams in the Bonda villages are very carefully maintained.

For G.N. Devy, development means to become free and fearless. He says, "To bring about development doesn't mean to acquire more consumer goods or to gain more wealth.... True development is which comes from within" (Devy, 2011: 133). Similar thoughts are expressed in the words of Pratibha Ray when she talks about civilization. I quote from the novel:

> What is the measure of civilization? Clothes, housing, and a mask to cover your face! ... Was civilization the body's covering, or the hearth's attire? Well, whatever it might be! Bodies could be clothed in a single day but it took centuries to dress hearts. It takes more than a government project to civilize hearts, but clothing people is easier. (Ray, 2001: 163)

It would be grossly incorrect to say that all the development projects taken up by the government to 'uplift' the tribes of Koraput hill and to 'civilize' them from the stage of 'barbaric, uncivilized and cruel situation' is totally meaningless and inappropriate. Instead it could be argued that the impact of these development projects is effective to a great extent in the areas of Koraput inhabited by the tribes. The so-called barbaric, naked and uneducated Bundas have started to wear clothes, have started to go to school and have accepted to involve themselves in the government projects to earn money. Though the writer is sarcastic when she talks about the Bonda's progress, her description definitely speaks volumes about the little development that the Bonda community has actually seen. "The electric lights, tube-wells, the tin-roofed houses of Indira Awas, the Bondunis in the Carpet Weaving Centre ... their long hair" (Ray, 2001: 268) are some definite steps in the way of progress of the tribes of the Bonda mountain.

Gradually, in the name of progress and development, the Bondas are separated from Nature. The word 'remo' means man, and in the Bonda community,

> [t]he remo falls from the yong's womb into the Earth Mother's lap clutching hunger and death in his fist. That is why he cries from the moment of birth. And from the moment it is the mother or the Earth that nourishes him. (Ray, 2001: 297)

Such is the attachment between the Bonda and his roots, between him and Mother Earth. Therefore, 'development and progress' of the Bonda tribe is a delicate and sensitive matter. Katu, a member of the Bonda tribe, protests against the government's attempt to make their women wear sari saying that "[i]f our women begin to wear clothes, the curse of the goddess will strike them" (Ray, 2001: 146). For the Bondas, wearing clothes could jeopardize the tribe's survival. Adibari, the first Bonduni women to wear sari has to face a lot of pain and suffering in her later life. Her reasons for deciding to wear a sari are very clear. She says, "I will wear a sari. If I wear a sari, the leader babu will give me a job. I will have money to feed myself and my mother" (Ray, 2001: 170). But at last she realizes that she has become a misfit in both the Bonda community and the educated community of the plains. The writer aptly remarks about Adibari: "Now she belonged neither to the mountain nor to the plains" (Ray, 2001: 187).

Further, the author mentions the beliefs of the Bondas regarding their women. The sari-wearing Bondunis, who had grown their hair long and are held up as models of progress, find themselves unwanted by the male members of their society.

> They were refusing to marry the educated Bonda youths, while the illiterate Bondas refused to marry them. Progress and education were conspiring to create a new class of Bonda men and women—those who were forced to remain single. (Ray, 2001: 224)

Somra, the youth from the Bonda tribe who studies in the government school is nowhere happy. He expresses his feelings to his friend Mangla:

> I am not happy in school and I am not happy here.... There, everyone makes fun of me, treats me with contempt; here, I find everyone wild, uncivilized. Everyone here is an object of charity, living on the government's scraps! We cannot speak out! (Ray, 2001: 235)

Somra's identity is at stake as if he belongs nowhere. He feels trapped in his shirt and shorts. When he returns to the village, he does not look like a Bonda. He can neither laugh, dance, drink or shout in rage nor can he walk about 'half-naked' like a Bonda. It has already been argued that the rhetoric of development has paved the way for civilizing missions in India. But we must admit the fact that at the same time it has radically altered the lifestyles, beliefs and views of that particular group on which the development schemes are recklessly practised. Therefore, to bring about positive changes in the lives of people, one has to change his/her approach to development. As Amita Baviskar (2005: 7) says,

> Deprivation is not a natural state for adivasis; it is produced and reproduced by the policies and practices that characterize India's post-colonial development. The landscape that adivasis inhabit has been the internal frontier for an expanding Indian economy—a source of minerals and timber, a site for mines, dams and heavy industries, and they have experienced the resultant erosion of their agriculture and forest-based economy.

Pratibha Ray's rendering of the socio-cultural life of the Bondas is feminist. She takes a critical view of the repressive nature of both the ancestral patriarchal tradition as well as the one imposed from the outside. In both the traditions, women are subjected to various forms of exploitation. In the traditional Bonda society that Ray depicts, the bride is supposed to take care of both the child-groom as well as the fields. The health of a family very often depends solely on the health of the mother who is expected to be equally 'productive' at home and in the fields. On the other hand, the advent of the outsiders to the Bonda hills brings about more effective and harsher forms of exploitation. The most serious affront on the dignity of the Bonda women is made by the outsiders who attempt to dress her up in the manner of 'civilized' women.

The intrinsic connection between the exploitation of nature and the exploitation of tribal people is also seen in the writings of Mahasweta Devi, a well-known name in Bengali literature. She has over a hundred books to her credit, including novels, story collections, children's book, and collections of plays. She has been a regular contributor to several magazines such as *Bortika* (a journal dedicated to the cause of oppressed communities within India). Her novel *Aranyer Adhikar* (Rights of the Forest) was published in 1977, and it is based on the life of Birsa Munda, a freedom fighter who belonged to a tribe. She has been a long-time champion for the political, social and economic advancement of the tribes of India. She has also donated the prize money from the Jnanapith and Magsaysay awards for the welfare of the tribes and continues to use her work to further the status of these groups in India. This activism is central to Devi's understanding of the role of a writer in society, as she believes a creative writer should have a social conscience and he/she should have a duty towards the society.

In an interview with Gabrielle Collu in Kolkata on 11 February 1997, Mahasweta Devi said:

> ...for the first time when I wrote that book on Birsa Munda (*Aranyer Adhikar*) ... they said that for the first time they got their place in history. Indian history did not recognize the tribal fights, tribal rebellions. Never recognized them. Never wrote about them. Never mentioned them. (Sen and Yadav, 2008: 227)

Aranyer Adhikar is the account of the life and times, thoughts, struggles and deeds of Birsa Munda, a mass leader of the 19th century. Devi was awarded Sahitya Akademi award for this novel in 1979. Moreover, she has been awarded Padma Shri in 1986, the Jnanpith award in 1996, Ramon Magsaysay award in 1997 and Padma Vibhushan in 2006 by the Government of India. She is said to be

> [a] committed writer in the sense that she has brought out the rebellious spirit of the tortured people of the past and the present with a rare blending of facts with fiction. Familarity with the documents, fidelity to her experiences ... mark her fiction as human documents of lasting value. (George, 1997: 89)

Her *Aranyer Adhikar* marked the beginning of her lifelong engagement with the tribal people and their right over the forest lands. The struggle in the novel is about the forest not only because the tribes have sustained themselves on the forest as a source of their livelihood but also for their close relationship with it. In the introduction to the book *Mahasweta Devi: An Anthology of Recent Criticism*, the editors have aptly stated that:

> This was a contract with one's environments, imbued with religious sentiments and expressed in mythical terms; it was the basis of their exclusivity against the outside world of the land pilfering *dikus*. (Sen and Yadav, 2008: 27)

Diku is a word that the tribes of the Chhotanagpur area use for the outsiders, mainly for the class of exploiters belonging to the Hindu mainstream society. Interestingly, in *Adibhumi* too, the Bonda tribe uses a word *gulang babu* for the outsiders who come to them as government officer.

Though the story of the novel starts with Birsa's death on June 1900, it goes back to his past life and the making of him as a leader. The vast areas of Chhotanagpur gradually go into the hands of *jotedars* or landowners, and the Mundas become bonded labourers. With the advent of moneylenders, zamindars, missionaries, government officers and the police, and with the construction of roads and railways, the old patterns of life undergo a thorough change.

Aranyer Adhikar is basically about a colonial peasant uprising, a revolt of the tribes launched against the British regime in the Chhotanagpur area. The novel talks about the member of a tribe as "a colonial subject who was doubly colonized first by the mainstream, dominantly Hindu caste society which sought to occupy forest and agricultural land belonging ancestrally to the tribes" (Sen and Yadav, 2008: 26). Over and above that, the British administration expands land revenue system to the belt of the tribes which created further troubles and difficulties for them.

Birsa Munda's father is Sugana Munda, and for him it has become difficult to remain in his ancestral village, where most of the cultivable land has been forcibly taken away by the moneylenders. Therefore, he had to move from one place to another and ultimately settles in his maternal ancestral village. Birsa feels and understands how hard his family has to toil for its livelihood. He tries to help his family in every way possible. Birsa is an excellent flute player, and playing his flute he roams about in the mountaneous forests. Often he feels that the two founder-fathers of Chhotanagpur are coming across the flooded river, and the black, virgin, forest-goddess, stretching both her hands on all sides in the midst of the flashes of lightning is shouting to them, "All this land is ours" (Devi, 2001b: 23).

The Mundas are so close to the forest that they cannot think of a life without it. So when Birsa is told by Ananda Pandee that the Mundas are not allowed to enter the forest and his parents cannot gather seeds and China grass for their meal, he is very frustrated and furious.

He enters deep inside the forest and hears the forest goddess crying, "The forest is raped by the *dikus*; it is imprisoned in the hands of law. Save me Birsa, I want to be pure and stainless" (Devi, 2001b: 63).

Birsa touches the ground, rubs his body against the trees and promises Mother Earth that he will make the forest pure and stainless. He exclaims in pain and says,

> You are the mother of all the Mundas. We, the Mundas get everything from you ... from you, we get the roof of our houses, the walls of our houses, the fruits in hunger, the rabbits, the porcupines, and the flesh of the birds ... everything. (Devi, 2001b: 63)

Birsa calls himself *dharti abba* (the father of the earth) as he considers it his duty to save and protect the earth from the alien invaders. The most significant point to note is that all the Mundas of the Chalkar area are in search of such a God, a new God who talks differently from the old gods whom they worshipped.

> They were not happy with the God who fascinated them with the fairy tales of spirit and who talked about the 'kingdom of heaven' in front of the hungry people. They were in search of a new God who would tell them not to kill the evil spirit but to kill the *dikus* and the government ... and who would tell them to snatch one's own right from whosoever it was. (Devi, 2001b: 68)

Mahasweta Devi has used fiction not only to resurrect the forgotten episodes of India's feudal past but to highlight the acts of local resistance against aggression and oppression. Devi's protagonist Birsa Munda wages a massive war against the British regime. After the suppresion of the first uprising, Birsa gives a clarion call to the Mundas (his followers) of a decisive war against the British. He names his new war as *ulgulan*. The Ulgulan movement creates panic in the hearts of the moneylenders, landlords, contractors, missionaries and the British imperialists. And it gives back to the adivasis their self-respect, teaches them to fight fearlessly and gives a new meaning to their lives. Birsa is a religious reformer and an agitator for the raiyats' forest and other rights, but eventually he aims at the political emancipation of the Munda area as well.

Birsa uses the myths and symbols of his society and culture, and becomes a rallying point for people to rise against foreign oppression and injustice. His movement is also infused with the spirit of religious reform, social justice and cultural regeneration. Though converted into Christianity during his schooling in a Christian mission school, in his later life he denounces Christianity realizing the colonial connection attached with it. Birsa Munda leads his men to rise against the imperial government and its policies. He and his followers, armed with bows and arrows, attack the British regiments and landlords, and reclaim what has been taken away from them. Modern-day civilization has looted them of everything they possessed; it chopped down their trees, took away their lands, minerals and made a mockery of their age-old rituals and customs. With the advent of heavy engineering and industry, and in spite of all the natural resources, the region continues to be one of the poorest and economically most underdeveloped region.

Mahasweta Devi has been a relentless critic of the development that wreaks havoc on the lives of indigenous people by severing their organic and symbiotic relationship with the forest. In her hands, Birsa Munda comes alive once again as a living symbol of the resistance of the subaltern. Though a 'cultural outsider' if the idea is too narrowly conceived, Mahasweta Devi recreates history from below, and she locates herself within the community. A social activist who has devoted her life to the cause of the adivasis, Devi's account of the failure of the colonial state to respect social and cultural differences is hard hitting and forceful. She is driven by the passion to bring to the fore the hero who, till then at least, was missing from the pages of Indian history. In the fiction that she has subsequently written, Mahasweta Devi has displayed an equal degree of anguish at the plight of the subaltern in the postcolonial state.

> Focusing on the recent questions of the extinction of the tribal people and their culture, Mahasweta Devi writes on the lives of these poor and indigenous Indians.... Without thinking of the consequences, we exploit the nature and natural resource and have an anthropocentric pride. Our hubristic denial of subaltern rights exposes our weakness as a modern man. (Rathod, 2013: 50)

The legacy of the colonial masters has been continued by the present-day rulers who have become bearers of the 'burden' of the white man that Rudyard Kipling so passionately asked his countrymen to take up. Pratibha Ray explores the continued story of negligence of the Bondas by both the British and the Indian 'masters' in a single novel. Through the character of Soma Muduli, she presents us with a character who has been through it all. She underscores the policy of both the colonial and the postcolonial state, more particularly of the latter, to measure the Bonda's relationship with the forest in terms of money. However, the fact that the value of a *salap* tree for a Bonda cannot be measured in terms of money or that the 'civilizing' mission of the state only helps to foster distrust and enmity amongst members of the tribe is conveniently ignored. Along with this, Pratibha Ray is successful in depicting the structures of repression, primarily the patriarchal structures that are already in existence in the society. These ancestral forms of oppression probably facilitate the 'colonization' mission.

Yeshe Dorjee Thongchi sets his story of love against the backdrop of a newly independent India when the process of development had just been initiated by the Indian state. Formerly ignored by the British through its policy of non-intervention in these lands, the Indian state, in spite of the apprehensions of the then prime minister whose remarks I quoted at the beginning of the chapter, takes up developmental activities, primarily centring around the construction of roads. In the world of Thongchi, these roads help to build bridges amongst the tribes who initially are suspicious of each other. However, at the same time, this exuberance is accompanied by a deep sense of unease which makes Thongchi apprehensive about the unrest and dissatisfaction that awaits the inhabitants of the North-East Frontier Agency once the road comes up.

To conclude, let me quote from Kalpana Bardhan's introduction to the collection of short stories entilted *Of Women, Outcasts, Peasants and Rebels*:

> The forms of oppression and resistance are particularly complex in a society in which the traditional hierarchies of age, sex, and caste have combined with increasing class stratification. In a context that combines

the oppression of feudalism (agrarian, patriarchal) with the exploitation of land, capital, organizational power, and the means of coercion, it is practically impossible to separate economic exploitation from sociocultural exploitation. (1990: 34)

In the case of all the writers under discussion, it is seen that they reflect a deep-seated sense of fear and suspicion of the impact of development programmes of the nation-state on the indigenous people. The fear of the indigenous culture and the indigenous ways of life being replaced by an alien culture and an alien way of life is uniform—whether it be Yeshe Dorjee Thongchi, Pratibha Ray or Mahasweta Devi. However, these writers also reveal the fact that "ethnicity must be viewed as a plastic and malleable social construction, deriving its meanings from the particular situations of those who invoke it ... Ethnicity has no essence or center, no underlying features or common denominator" (Smith, 1998: 204). Thus, while Yeshe Dorjee Thongchi reflects on the identity politics that beset the North East of India, Pratibha Ray emphasizes the marginalization of the indigenous tribes by a process of colonization that was initiated by the British but continued in the post-Independence phase by the machineries of the Indian state that failed to take into account the different understandings of the relationship between the tribes and their lands. To some extent, Pratibha Ray's concerns are also manifest in Mahasweta Devi's, but the latter's understanding of ethnicity is informed by a class-based exploitation of the marginalized people. Thus, what does one understand by ethnicity is contingent on the geo-political area where the question is raised. It may be pertinent to ask here why in the North East of India competition for resources has centred on issues of ethnicity rather than class struggle. Bates's interpretation of "ethnic group formation" as the result of "dynamic and rational behavior" and as an "attempt to deal with, organize, and benefit from the modernization of societies" (1974: 475) is particularly useful to understand the situation in North East India.

4
Folkloric Materials in Ethnic Novels (With Special Reference to Narayan, Rong Bong Terang, Lummer Dai, Yeshe Dorjee Thongchi and Sishuram Pegu)

Every literary work bears the stamp of culture. This is true both when the author writes about his culture or when he writes about a culture that he has studied, lived and experienced. The author creates out of what he knows, what he experiences and what he is familiar with; to express this in terms of poststructuralist philosophy, one could say that the author creates out of what has 'always already' existed. Every society has various traditional beliefs, customs, legends and myths which play a vital role in shaping the perspectives of the inhabitants of these societies. One only needs to pay a cursory glance at the vast number of stories that were written and, in fact, continue to be written in India, the origins of which can be traced to the *Ramayana* and the *Mahabharata*. The lives and the actions of people are powerfully influenced by folk beliefs and customs. Ethnographic novels attempt to reflect the reality of the communities. These fictions signify the relationship between the individual and his/her society.

While trying to analyse the essentials that enter into the creation of literature, we have to understand the use of folklore in literature. It would be appropriate to quote Thomas Wolfe (1943: xxix) in this context:

If the writer has used the clay of life to make his book, he has only used what all men must, what none can keep from using. Fiction is not fact, but fiction is fact selected and understood, fiction is fact arranged and charged with purpose. Dr. Jonhson remarked that a man would turn over half a library to make a single book; in the same way, a novelist may turn over half the people in a town to make a single figure in his novel.

Paul A. Bennett, in his article 'Folklore and the Literature to Come' (1952: 23), discusses three distinct relationships of folklore to literature. For him, folklore can be used (a) directly as literature, (b) in a modified form of literature, and (c) as a plane of reference in the production of literature. A creative writer uses folkloric materials in literature in a modified form. And he/she collects the materials from various sources. I would like to quote Bennett (1952: 23) here:

> ...the learning of the folk, the knowledge of an untutored people made one by geography, occupation or culture—or by a combination of the three—supplies a great body of raw materials for the creative artist. The particular value of folklore as raw material is that it offers a tested pattern of appeal, the appeal of a striking character or a sure-fire treatment of love, lust or rage; of birth, life or death.

Literature can thus use folkloric materials such as folktales, folk beliefs, myths or legends for structuring a story as well as for thematic purposes; use of folklore in literature is however not limited to this: folklore can also be incorporated as characters or in the settings of the creative pieces. Adding this to the writer's own experiences, these materials provide a greater scope for fascinating and memorable stories. It is true that whatever materials the writer uses to create his works, he believes these to be the best. Conversely, he tries to arrange for the best available materials he has or he collects as these would provide some new experiences to the readers. In the name of new experiences, the writer cannot merely provide ethnographic details of a society. Mere ethnographic detail would make a literary piece aesthetically poor. The writer should be able to transform the ethnographic details in a sophisticated manner into something that has artistic craftsmanship. It is important for a creative writer to be acquainted with the technique of artistic use of folk materials in his writings. He should be able to serve a valuable literary purpose by using the folk materials in his writings.

Folklore offers new insights into our understanding of creative writing. It is believed that to analyse folklore in literature, there are certain methods. Among the different types of folklore, a few folk items have been discussed and analysed here in view of the settings and themes of the creative works. Among these, some items occupy a place of importance while others do not. According to Richard M. Dorson (1957: 3),

> ...proverbial sayings, expressions and similes rank first among the types of folklore extracted, probably because they are easiest to cull. Customs and folkways, superstitions and beliefs, come next; frontier humor, in the form of tall tales, boasts, hoaxes, and comic folktypes, follows; the use of folkloristic themes, like the Devils receives occasional attention; and at the bottom, surprisingly, fall the categories of folktale and folksongs.

Dorson put forward three arguments/methods to identify and analyse the relationship of a given work with the folk tradition which I think would be appropriate to mention here. He believes that an author can be shown through biographical evidence to have enjoyed direct contact with oral lore. Secondly he says,

> Besides biographical information, a second technique available to the folk critic proceeds from *internal evidence* in the literary composition itself that indicates direct familiarity of the author with folklore. This evidence includes the alleged folktales, folksongs, folk sayings or folk customs embedded in literature as well as their settings. (1957: 7)

His third method asks for something more than mere biographical information and folklore "woven naturally into the speech and manners of regional characters". Moreover, he "must prove that the saying, tale, song or custom inside the literary work possess an independent traditional life ... [it] must present *corroborative evidence* to supplement his proofs from biographical and internal evidence" (1957: 7).

These methods would help one to identify and analyse the presence of folklore in literature. In my study here, I would like to analyse the folkloric materials used by the ethnographic writers thus bringing these methods into active consideration. While identifying folk beliefs, traditional customs and superstitions in a literary piece of an ethnographic writer, we can never overlook the time and place in which the text is produced. Folk belief is a matter of common belief to a larger extent in certain communities at a certain period of time. As such, it is not unnatural that the literature produced at that time by the people of that community is lighted up by the representation of folk beliefs and practices of that community.

Folk beliefs and customs are related to the traditional belief systems that are believed in and practised by people and are therefore used in fictional writings. Folk beliefs and folk customs form an important part of folk literature, providing a cohesive force to the community at large. At the same time, these act as a record of ethno-history. Man is a social being by nature, and always strives for a kind of identity, the identity belonging to a group, to a community or to a society. Folk beliefs are catalytic agents that enhance this very sense of identity and thus aid the process of ethnicity formation. They provide a base for social solidarity.

There are three formulas for the adaptation of particular folk elements into formal literature: (a) function and form may remain constant, (b) perpetuation of the form of a folk tradition whose function has changed since the time of its oral currency, and (c) reflection of altered function by modification of form (Haffman, 1957: 19). Daniel G. Haffman in his 'Folklore in Literature: Notes towards a Theory of Interpretation' discusses the use of folk material in literature. He believes that critics are concerned with the function of the folk materials in their cultural contexts. It is believed that folk-materials contribute to the qualities of the literary texts in which these are incorporated. Folklore contributes to the plot, setting and character of a particular literary text. In addition, he wonders if the writer's debt to folklore is for "traditional patterns ... the structure, the symbol" as well (Gillmor, quoted in Haffman, 1957: 20).

We can trace three levels of significance in the literary uses of folk materials. In the very first place, the introduction of folkloric materials is just to provide verisimilitude to a depiction of the life of a particular locality. The use of folklore in this sense is very much regional. The second level is that proposed by Coffin. It combines many folkloristic elements. Here is the use of folk materials in their most significant contribution to literature, as a source of structural symbols. Quoting Haffman (1957: 21) again:

> If we are interested in what folklore offers literature as a repository of shared social symbols, conserving important cultural values in incipient dramatic or literary form, then our separate concerns folklorist, historians, and critics of literature will lead us to studies mutually enriching.

Chinua Achebe, the African novelist, believes that cultures use folklore to pass on great cultural richness. He believes that folklore can provide solutions to people's questions and problems. Folklore, being an important feature of ethnic cultures, finds ample and appropriate place in ethnographic fiction. Achebe's own fiction feeds on oral traditions of his culture. He makes ample use of myths and legends and other folkloric materials. He explores devices of oral traditions for the purpose of their preservation and also for teaching moral values of folk wisdom. Achebe's first novel *Things Fall Apart* is said to be the first novel rendering a complete account of the African tribal life.

> Achebe's Africa was neither the heart of darkness, nor an anthropological case-study; it was a human world inhabited by beings that a reader of any race or nationality could identify with and understand. (Lindfors, 1972: 213)

While analyzing an ethnographic novel, it is important to know for whom it is written and to whom it is addressed. If it is written to address his own people, the writer neither has to translate the community-specific words nor does he have to give footnotes for the culture-specific words. But if the writer wants to address the community beyond his own, he has a tendency to add new words, proverbs, folktales, metaphors, beliefs, customs and traditions and oral lore in his creative work. The explanation of tribal beliefs and customs in an aesthetic way is the result of the creative genius in a writer. Achebe possessed that creative genius in him which enabled him to weave proverbs, folktales and traditional oral lore into the fabric of his fictions.

In this chapter I will discuss the reflection of folk beliefs and customs in the novel *Kocharethi* by Narayan, *Rongmilir Hanhi* by Rong Bong Terang, *Mon aru Mon* by Lummer Dai, *Sava Kota Manuh* by Yeshe Dorjee Thongchi and *Dhansiri Ganwar Dekajan* (The Young

Man from the Dhansiri Village) by Sishuram Pegu. The beliefs and rituals, customs and traditions of the Malayarayar tribe of Kerala, the Karbis of Assam, the Adis of Arunachal Pradesh, the Monpas of the West Kameng District of Arunachal Pradesh and the Misings of the Bokakhat region of Assam are depicted in these novels. While writing about the lives and societies of these extremely diverse groups of ethnic communities, the novelists succeed in creating ethnographic fiction instead of writing mere ethnographic notes. And having said this, I restate a point that I had made earlier even at the risk of being repetitive—the relationship between literature and society is never direct and simple. Even the fiction written in the tradition of 19th century realistic fiction did carry the ideological baggage of the author. If the relationship between literature and life had been as direct as it is sometimes assumed, there would have been no difference between literary and other kinds of writing.

I am aware that in many cases the act of writing fiction may be an assertion of a particular cultural identity. And the use of folk beliefs and customs in fiction can be seen as a strategy for resisting the hegemony of the dominant culture. This dominant culture may be European colonialism or Indian colonialism. In some ethnic novels, it is obvious that the author writes with the idea of introducing the readers to the diverse cultural materials of the society about which he writes. And if the author 'belongs' to that particular community, he seems to be informative instead of idealistic, not romanticizing everything ethnic as 'exotic' or 'strange' (Misra, 2001: 33).

In the novel *Dhansiri Ganwar Dekajan*, Sishuram Pegu depicts the picture of the Mising community living near the river. The customs and traditions, beliefs and rituals of a traditional Mising village are very well wrought into the subject matter of the novel. In the *Ali Aye Ligang* festival, the Mising people observe several rituals. All these rituals are described in the novel when the villagers celebrate the festival (Pegu, 2006: 50). Similarly, Pegu introduces us to the *Po-rag* festival and the rituals associated with it. He describes how the Mising youths get involved in the preparation of the local wine *chai apong* on a specific date before *Po-rag* or in decorating the *murung ghar* with colourful drawings and taking part in the *gumrag* dance. The works and activities of the festival are divided among the villagers systematically. There are some positions such as *borpuwari, migam bora, deka bora, tiri bora* and all of these, as seen in the novel, are assigned different tasks in the festivals.

While stating the detailed description of the customs, rituals or festivals of the Mising community, we feel that the novelist is keen to showcase his culture and tradition to the wider readership while at the same time there is the urge to assert his cultural identity. When he talks about *purang apong* (rice packed in a special kind of leaf), *ni-tom* (song) or *saglen, rugbad, so-man* and *chai apong* and explains the meaning of each of these community-specific words, the readers are drawn into the cultural life of the Mising community. By giving details of his culture, Pegu tries to establish and secure both his personal identity as a member of the Missing community as well as the identity of the community.

Rong Bong Terang expresses a similar view while answering a question about the inspiration behind the creation of *Rongmilir Hanhi*. He says:

> My dream had always been to introduce the land and the people of Karbi Anglong to the outside world. *Rongmilir Hanhi* became the medium to make that dream come true. (Goswami, 2012)

Narayan's *Kocharethi* is marked by the same urge. With five novels and two collections of short stories, Narayan is generally acclaimed to be the first novelist of South India belonging to a tribe. He is the recipient of the prestigious Kerala Sahitya Akademi award. In fact, *Kocharethi* is the first novel in Malayalam to be written by someone who belongs to the Malayarayar tribe. The novel is based on the culture and history of the Malayarayar tribe which inhabits the Western Ghats in Kerala. The myths, rituals, social customs and belief systems of the Malayarayar tribe and their struggle for possession of land are documented in the novel.

Steeped in the oral tradition of an Adivasi society, Narayan unfolds the Malayarayars' changing perceptions of land and its ownership and documents a life that is slowing fading into history. The first half of the novel focuses on belief systems, rituals and various social codes of the Malayarayar tribe. G.S. Jayasree writes in the introduction of the translated version of *Kocharethi*:

> The first half of the novel is an ethnohistorian's delight, with particulars of beliefs and rituals unique to a set of people who live in close communion with nature. The various social or cultural codes—'verbal codes' ... 'bodily codes' ... 'commodity codes' ... and 'behavioural codes' ... are detailed minutely. (Narayan, 2011: xvii)

Jayasree further says that rituals are ingrained in the cultural ethos of the ethnic groups and are passed on from one generation to the next. A unique set of rituals—'life cycle rituals'—marking birth ceremonies, marriage customs, and funeral services that help in the assimilation of the individual into the social fabric of that community are observed by the Malayarayars. There is elaborate mention of the observance of social taboos related to the days of menstruation. The taboos attached with the menstruation and childbirth are 'conspicuous' (Narayan, 2011: xx). In the Malayarayar community, the menstruating woman and the pregnant lady has to live in an *eettappera* (a shack). To quote from the text:

> The *eettappera* was close to the house—a one-room structure to which a woman withdrew when she was menstruating or about to give birth. A menstruating woman confined herself to that room for seven days, during those days, she would not enter the kitchen, would not appear in the frontyard of the house or touch anyone.... Food would be brought to the *eettappera* and served on a leaf.... When she went out of the room, she took great care not to touch any men or boys even by accident. (Narayan, 2011: 34)

The novel *Mon aru Mon* by Lummer Dai too includes a variety of folk beliefs and traditional customs of the Adi society which are either described by the narrator or observed by the characters of the novel. *Mon aru Mon* is set against the backdrop of the Adi society. The Adi is a tribe of Arunachal Pradesh living in the East, West and Upper Siang districts and part of Dibang Valley and Upper Subansiri districts of the state. In the first page of the novel we are introduced to an Adi belief:

> Lakhimi Devi is angry with me as I could not offer my worship during the Solung festival due to illness. (Dai, 1967: 1; my translation)

Gidum, the widow-protagonist could not offer worship in the Adi festival *Sulung*, and she believes that the scarcity of rice is a result of the anger of the goddess of wealth. Similarly, Malayarayars believe that the gods keep close watch over them; they consider natural calamities to be the sign of the anger of ancestral spirits for wrongdoings. It is also believed that spirits can possess a person as in the case of Kadutha, and Ittyadi tries to drive out the spirit by thrashing him.

It is interesting that in the novel *Mon aru Mon*, grandmother Gidum firmly believes that Dadam is possessed by *Ngippong Wiyu* (goddess who is responsible for killing women in childbirth). Gidum believes that *Ngippong* entered the body of Dadam, so she beats her with a bunch of leaves that causes an itching sensation in order to chase *Ngippong* away.

Lummer Dai introduces the readers to the belief associated with the *ari* (the stillborn baby or the baby that dies immediately after birth). The *gam* of the village declares, "No one should leave the village" (Dai, 1967: 2). In the Adi society, no one can leave the village or cross the river for five days if someone from the village passes away (Dai, 1967: 95). When Gidum asks what has happened, she is told that Dadam has given birth to a stillborn child. And Gidum automatically infers that no one is supposed to leave the village or be engaged in any work as this might harm him/her. Moreover, Gidum finds a relation between Dadam's misfortune (giving birth to a stillborn child) and her being involved in the act of yarning when a tiger attacked Gamuk. Thus, one folk belief leads to another: if someone yarns at the time when someone else of the same village is being attacked by a tiger, he/she has to face dire consequences. Dadam's giving birth to an *ari* strengthens grandmother Gidum's faith in this belief.

Lummer Dai, being a pioneering writer of Arunachal Pradesh, is a first-generation literate, coming originally from rural Arunachal, and therefore, appears to have a deep knowledge and close sense of affiliation with this rural society. It is this sense of affiliation that makes him include so many Adi beliefs, rituals and traditions in his fictional world.

Folk beliefs are important for an understanding of the society and culture in which these are rooted. In fact, an analysis of folk beliefs of a society can unfold the conceptual machinery of values, beliefs and social arrangement, including the social structure of that society.

Moreover, we feel that in the use of such beliefs and customs there is always a tendency on the part of the novelist to document the fast disappearing ways of life of the community to which he/she belongs. Perhaps Narayan took up writing about his community as it is believed that those who belong outside the community take the license to idealize, romanticize or distort its beliefs and practices. In her introduction to *Kocharethi,* Jayasree says that in Narayan's words such representations tended to depict the Adivasi as a monochromatic figure, like a demon of mythological story. And in her view, Narayan gives us an authentic picture, the story told by one who has lived the life that he depicts (Narayan, 2011: xvii). In this context she quotes Narayan:

> We wanted to tell the world that we have our own distinctive ways of life, our own value system. We are not demons lacking in humanity but a strong, hardworking and self-reliant community. (Narayan, 2011: xvii)

There are specific death rituals of the Malayarayars and the Adis and these are observed by the characters of the novels. In *Kocharethi,* the relatives of the dead have to observe *pula* or death-related ritual that necessitates quarantining. *Pula* is to be observed for fifteen days, during which period it is taboo to touch weapons, to enter the cultivated land, to perform any rites or to appear before idols. Liquor and contact with woman is also strictly forbidden. On the fifteenth day, a ritual bath and on the sixteenth day, a festive meal for relatives and friends is organized. Similarly, in *Mon aru Mon*, we come across many beliefs and rituals related to death.

It is significant to note that though in all the above-mentioned novels, there are ample evidences of folk beliefs and strict observance of these beliefs and rituals, a set of characters do defy norms of adherence to traditional customs and rituals. As a result, the clash between tradition and modernity is also reflected in the novels.

For anyone who is unacquainted with the customs of the Monpa tribe living in the easternmost province of Arunachal Pradesh, a reading of the Assamese novel *Sava Kota Manuh* would introduce a belief system that is far removed from the realities of their life. In fact, in a way, the novelist welcomes the readers to be 'culturally shocked' at the beginning and thereby succeeds in sustaining their interest right through. However, as the readers discover later, the novel is much more than a mere representation of a traditional practice that to dispassionate outsiders might seem to be exotic. In fact, not only does the novel transport us to the divine world of Buddhist spirituality and religion, it also raises fundamental questions regarding the manoeuvring of cultural 'facts' by the fictional writer to shape, and even to challenge, the reader's understanding of what is 'normative behaviour'.

The most important theme of the novel *Sava Kota Manuh* (as per the author's statement in the preface) is the prevalent Monpa custom of cremating the body of the dead by slicing it into a hundred and eight pieces and then throwing these pieces into the river. The customs and rituals of a society constitute the belief in some ideological order that one internalizes as a social being. These are social constructs and the member of a particular society is a product of such social construction. The Monpa's belief that slicing a dead body is as good as going on pilgrimage (Thongchi, 2004: 31) is as much a social construction as the belief of the reader who looks at such a custom with abhorrence. Yeshe Dorjee Thongchi's novel plays on this conflict between these two belief systems, drawing on both to problematize the location of the writer himself within any one system.

Ideology takes such deep root in Ao Thampa that even if he wants to leave this job, he is unable to do so as he firmly believes that it is a sin to say 'no' to such a divine calling. Aane Sangge's words, "Cremate the dead body respectfully. See to it that the dead body is cut into the stipulated number of parts" (Thongchi, 2004: 219; my translation) is an indication of her ingrained belief in her tradition. The irony is that the custom of slicing the dead bodies is considered to be a holy work, but the man involved in it is not a 'normal' human being, unhappy in his familial life and his daughter is physically challenged. Ao Thampa remembers his mother's words, "His mother warned him not to be a *thampa*, a man who slices dead bodies. The belief that through the sacred work of slicing dead bodies one can earn salvation is proven to be untrue in his life" (Thongchi, 2004: 41; my translation). This is perhaps an expression of the author's sense of scepticism in such traditional beliefs.

Ao Thampa throws up on the first day of his profession as he sees his hands, feet and his whole body soaked with puss and pieces of rotten meat. The same man later becomes practical enough to be able to slice dead bodies with full attention in a matter-of-fact manner. The description of slicing the dead body of his uncle Meme Chorgen Karma Thingle into a hundred and eight pieces evokes an authentic picture:

> At first the two legs were cut and then floated in the river. This was followed by the hands. The body without the hands and legs and the head looked like a sack full of flour. What a dreadful sight! There was no blood in it as it was kept for three days and three nights after death. Instead there was a foul smelling puss of a reddish-black colour.... The foul smell of rotten flesh filled the place. (Thongchi, 2004: 84; my translation)

It is significant to note that towards the end of *Sava Kota Manuh*, the *thampa* gives up the work of slicing dead bodies; he becomes 'clean', 'rational' and 'natural', and in the author's own words a 'good' human being (Thongchi, 2004: 126).

The religious note is the most important concern of the novel *Sava Kota Manuh*. The Monpas are Buddhists by religion. As such, while the setting of the novel is based on a traditional custom of the Monpa tribe, it automatically demands reference to rituals and beliefs of the religion followed by them. The Tawang *gompa*, the second biggest Buddhist monastery in the world, the Lamas, the Dalai Lama, the Rimpoche are images and ideas closely associated with Buddhism that are used frequently in the novel. We are introduced to the religious rituals of the Monpas when we are informed about the pilgrimage that Darge and Rijomba used to embark on; for Darge and Rijomba, the most pleasurable time is to go on pilgrimage to the Tawang *gompa* or to Khinmay, Urgaling, Changbu, Thungmen, Brahmaduchung *gompa*, etc. (Thongchi, 2004: 24). The mention of *nekor* (pilgrimage), *wang* (blessings), *kurim* (worship), and the *torgya* festival conveys the religious belief of the Buddhists. The Monpas' belief in Dalai Lama, His reincarnation and His words as the ultimate truth is the reflection of their unflinching faith in Buddhism: *gelukpa*, *kringmapa* and *karmapa* are different sects of the Mahayana Buddhists, and the people belonging to these sects believe that to be born as a human being is the result of the good deeds of many previous births and that to be blessed with a sight of Dalai Lama is the reward of great devotion (Thongchi, 2004: 65–66).

The mantras written in the Tibetan language are beyond their understanding; still they are very sacred for them. All that is to be done can be easily materialised by reading such mantras. Moreover, it can heal both the physical and spiritual wounds; it can destroy the power of the evil spirit and can wash off all the sins of human beings leading to the salvation of the soul. (Thongchi, 2004: 70; my translation)

The Monpas also believe that when a Rimpoche is born in someone's house, some kind of untoward incident takes place in that house (Thongchi, 2004: 175). These beliefs mentioned in the novel reflect the author's sense of affinity to the religious beliefs of Buddhism as well as his deep attachment to the community very close to his own. Thongchi belongs to the Sherdukpen community, a community that has close ties with the Monpas.

Thongchi's novel tells us about the food habits of the Monpas, more particularly food items such as *jhan* and *churpi* that are offered to Ao Thampa by his wife. We also come to know about the Losar, the Torgya and the other festivals of the Monpas.

In 'Mor Sahitya Sarchar Bisoye Mor Baktabya' (My Views Regarding My Writings) (Thongchi, 2006: 10), the author talks about the deep sense of pain that he felt during the writing of *Sava Kota Manuh*. Thongchi does not elaborate the reasons behind the pain that he experienced while writing the novel. But we have reasons to believe that this pain could be the result of Thongchi's sense of scepticism regarding a custom prevalent in a tribe very close to his own.

Fiction can bring about a convergence between the universal and the local. Thongchi's *Sava Kota Manuh* illustrates such an act of convergence. The novelist chooses a particular custom of an ethnic community and on the basis of it he tries to depict the love between the *thampa* (the man involved in the task of slicing dead bodies) and the saint. The love between these two characters is not a hackneyed sentimental love affair between two youthful lovers, but a deep spiritual love.

The significant role of Buddhism in the Monpa society and the immense impact of the Chinese aggression are some important matters which constitute the subject matter of the novel. Towards the end of the novel, the novelist brings about a convergence of the particular and the general in the sense that though based on a particular social custom of a community, the novelist succeeds in transcending the narrow limits by introducing issues of religion and matters of social relevance. At the end, Ao Thampa's death by immersing himself in the river just after the performance of the death rituals of Aane Sangge is depicted in a manner that transports the readers to a different world. The Tawangchu river started to overflow when Ao Thampa placed the head of Aane Sangge on the particular stone placed for the purpose. He pronounced the mantra *Om mone peme hom* just before slicing the dead body of Aane Sangge. It is significant to note that even at the time of performing the custom of slicing dead bodies, he keeps chanting religious prayers. By depicting the death of Ao Thampa, the novelist tries to assimilate the universal with the local. The climactic scene presents the assimilation of the body in water and thereby introduces the idea of the purifying power of water in every religion.

The same idea finds expression in the novel *Mon aru Mon*. Though the novel is about a widow and her pet dog, Bomong, it is the story of the universal relationship between man and nature. Through elaborate description of various Adi beliefs and rituals, the novelist tries to paint a picture of the Adi society. At the same time, the inner void of humans and the eternal relationship of man to nature are presented in a very vivid manner.

Kocharethi too expresses the relationship between man and nature. In fact, in an interview with Catherine Thankamma, Narayan (2011: 216) said, "We, Arayars, are children of the hills". In the same interview Thankamma says that what struck her when she first read *Kocharethi* was the intimate link between the Araya community and the environment. She believes that Narayan began to write about environmental issues long before the world sat up and began to take notice (Narayan, 2011: 216).

In an interview with the translator, included at the end of the novel, Narayan (2011: 208–209) says that one of the reasons that prompted him to write this novel was the growing realization that creative writing was in the hands of the elite upper classes; the communities portrayed in those writings belonged to these classes. The Adivasi, when represented, appeared as a monochromatic figure. It was always a negative picture; he was depicted as apathetic, unable to react to injustice or worse, inhuman or sub-human, vicious. He existed for the sole purpose of being defeated and /or killed by the forces of virtue and goodness, represented by the upper castes.

In this context, postcolonialism provides us with useful tools to make sense of the political implications of retaining the local in the framework of the universal. Postcolonialism demonstrates the heterogeneity of colonized places by analyzing the uneven impact of Western colonialism on different places, peoples and cultures.

It is true that the Malayarayars, as depicted in *Kocharethi*, were geographically and culturally isolated from the 'civilized' world. But they were not on the whole free from outside authority. During the mid-19th century, several disturbing changes seem to have affected them. According to G.S. Jayasree,

> These were the consequence of a steady process of modernization introduced by the Travancore Government at the instance of British colonial administration. Large quantities of teak were required for shipbuilding and the laying of railway lines. For this, great stretches of land were forcefully taken from the Malayarayars leased out to European planters. (Narayan, 2011: xxv)

These changes not only led to a change in the mode of cultivation, but with different processes of modernization these changes introduced a host of other changes in the lives of the Malayarayars. With the road connection to the land of the Adivasi (that was secluded from external influences) many things entered. It opened the door to the Tamil merchants and encouraged cash economy. As a result, traditional perception of wealth underwent a change and materialism entered the Adivasi society. Towards the end of the novel, Narayan reveals his awareness of the clash between the forces of tradition and modernity.

Such a clash between tradition and modernity is very well depicted in Lummer Dai's novel *Mon aru Mon*. The lifestyles, thought processes and the reactions towards various objects, rituals or customs have been changing with the advent of education and as a result of modernization. Dai tries to show such changes through different characters of this novel. Ajong and Badang are two characters who stand in support of modernity unlike a traditional character like Gidum. Most of the characters in the novel talk of *koson puja, dotgang* (sacrificing pig or mithun in favour of the dead, it is believed that this pig or mithun becomes the servant of the soul of the dead) (Dai, 1967: 150) and of burying the horn of a buffalo to stop sunlight and to welcome rain (Dai, 1967: 141). Ajong and Badang constantly defy such social norms for the perceived betterment of society in the form of health facilities and education. The novelist's inner conflict is very well reflected in Badang's speech meant for Ajong:

> I am a creation of the old world. But the world in front of us is moving forward at a fast pace. And I am struggling in the vortex of the new and the old. (Dai, 1967: 118; my translation)

Close attachment to his society enables Dai to colour the traditional Adi social life in his novel *Mon aru Mon* with a variety of folk beliefs. But at the same time, the modern man in him makes him show Gidum being cured by medicines, not by *koson puja*. We hear the voice of the writer when Badang thinks:

> Grandmother Gidum will not be able to go to the field for three days as she has performed *koson puja*; she firmly believes that the *bondevata* will be dissatisfied if she does so. In this way the valuable time of many people is wasted. (Dai, 1967: 123; my translation)

Jitanjali Borpujari (1999: 61; my translation) rightly says, "Lummer Dai is successful in depicting a clear picture of eternal conflict between the new and the old."

Rong Bong Terang illustrates the socio-cultural aspects of the Karbi society in his novel *Rongmilir Hanhi*. The novelist tries to bring to light the changes taking place in the society as a result of different economic and political influences subsequent to the emergence of a commercial civilization. Saraik Terang is the *sarbasa* or the village-headman of the Rongmili village and is respected by everyone. He is rudely treated by the hunter Sarthe Teron, under the influence of the new commercial civilization. He is the chief judge or *habisek* and Saraik Terang is his subordinate. However, *sarbasa* Saraik Terang is more respected by the villagers than *habisek* Teron.

The plotting of a conspiracy against the honest, simple *sarbasa* by a dishonest, wicked and more powerful *habisek* is the main story of the novel. The villagers safeguard the house of the *sarbasa* and they manage to apprehend the guilty ones involved in the conspiracy. Saraik forgives his enemies who try to set his house on fire and burn it down to ashes. G.P. Sarma (2010) says,

> At the instigation of the local people, and the support of the royal ministers and the royal priests and other law keepers or *habeks*, hunter Teron is dismissed from his post of a *habisek*. Thus Rongmili smiles—an open, honest smile.

In Sarma's views, the virtues of the old, ancient Karbi society, and its simplicity, honesty and truthfulness are portrayed in the novel. Modern society brings in its wake the baggage of education, culture, knowledge and science which are inevitable for the progress of the Karbi society. However, the new civilization brought about by the influence of money, corruption, immorality and the lust for power prove to be a curse to the Karbi society. *Sarbasa* Saraik Terang is a character who represents all the virtues of the ancient Karbi society. He is not against the new educational progress of the children or the new generation of youths.

In *Rongmilir Hanhi*, a love story has been depicted and through it the social customs, rules and rituals, and the social ways of the Karbi people have been illustrated. The beautiful harmony and skillful handling of human situations have uplifted it from being a mere documentation of a fast disappearing way of life.

The most striking thing about the novel is the delineation of the life and culture of the Karbis in the colonial era; it depicts a people caught between the competing claims of old and new values. Like Narayan in *Kocharethi*, Rong Bong Terang does not show an insular ethnic community; he depicts the influence of external factors such as education, commerce, refugees from east Bengal and Nepal occupying Karbi land, the curse of opium, the conversion into Christianity and its impact on the life of Karbi people.

Terang presents a realistic picture of poverty in the Karbi society. The root cause of the acute poverty that afflicts the Karbis is believed to be opium. The addicts exchange mustard seeds, rice grains, sesame for opium. The trader of opium, known as *mahajan* (who is a non-Karbi, as in the novel, a Marwari trader), exploits the local people.

Lindok Terong is a victim of such addiction. He was a hardworking man earlier, but he fell for the lure of opium. We see his steady deterioration through the novel before his untimely death at the end of it.

It is not only the influence of opium that brought a remarkable change in the lives of the Karbi people, a significant change in the lifestyles and beliefs of the Karbi people is brought about by Christianity. In an article published in *Muse India*, Stuti Goswami (2012) rightly says:

> The Tikka hill on which stands the Christian mission was discovered by the American Baptist Missionary P.E. Moore and his assistant Carwell in the year 1896. Together they built a church in the dense hill, which was revered as the abode of gods of the Karbi community and this brought in a significant alteration in the Karbi Society—many Karbi families were converted into Christianity, and were settled in villages around Tikka hills.

However, the non-Christian Karbis considered the building of the church as a sign of disrespect to the traditional gods. It stimulated the popular belief that the gods were infuriated, and therefore, punished the people with poverty, hunger and death. It is important to note that Saroik Terang considers such beliefs to be superstitions.

There is a definite pattern in the selection of folk beliefs by the various writers under discussion. There is no doubt that the writers use the folk beliefs of various communities for assertion of a particular cultural identity, but it is unmistakably accompanied by an indecision regarding subscribing to these beliefs and customs. In each of the novels under discussion, it is observed that while a particular set of characters wholeheartedly follow the traditional beliefs, rituals and customs, another set of characters vehemently oppose the customs and rituals of the community and try to analyse the superstitions from the rational standpoint of modernity. This is true in the case of Rong Bong Terang's *Rongmilir Hanhi*, Lummer Dai's *Mon aru Mon*, Sishuram Pegu's *Dhansiri Ganwar Dekajan* and Narayan's *Kocharethi*. In *Kocharethi*, Parvati makes a departure from the traditional beliefs when she removes the black thread which she wore around her neck after her first menstruation. It is believed in the Malayayarar community that during *theendari* (periods), a girl is not supposed to touch books or visit far-off places. Parvati breaks all these norms and starts going to school even when she is having her periods.

I believe that this dilemma of the characters with regard to various folk beliefs or customs originates within the writer. The choices of particular folk beliefs over others certainly reveal the ideology of the writer. But the conflict in him is expressed through the use of folk beliefs and customs. The society is a battleground of the clash between tradition and modernity, between the old and the new, and the writer represents this clash through literature.

In this context, Professor Von Furer-Haimendorf (1977: 2) said something significant in response to a query in his own mind. He was curious to know why the tribes, who had lived in a state of complete self-sufficiency, developing their own way of life and cultural individuality without any need for outside assistance, now has to be protected and aided by the government. He finds the answer for this:

> The simple answer is that through no fault of their own many tribal groups had their traditional style of life disrupted by alien populations who invaded their habitat and introduced the paraphernalia of a technologically advanced civilization incompatible in many of its aspects with the basic orientation of the indigenous culture.

The situation is similar in almost all the tribes of India (may be in other parts of the world too). There are references to the disruption of the ethnic lifestyle by the outsiders in Rong Bong Terang's *Rongmilir Hanhi* and Narayan's *Kocharethi*. Narayan (2011: 212) says:

> The Christians came and started English medium schools. They said worshipping stones and trees was wrong. Then the Rashtriya Swayamsevak Sangh (RSS) and Vishwa Hindu Parishad (VHP) came and did the same—replaced Puliambulli and Marutha with Vishnu and Durga; ochre robes replaced the gowns of the priests and nuns. No one was really interested in us as a people.

The conversion into Christianity brought about a remarkable change in the lives and societies of the ethnic people. Rong Bong Terang expresses this change through the character of Habejan. On one occasion Habejan says,

> After the coming of the missionaries no traditional customs or rituals of the Karbis of the Tikka region is alive. There is no name of *peng-sojun*, no

traditional songs and dances and even the death-rituals are disappearing. (Terang, 1993: 40; my translation)

It is true that an author's ideology gets reflected in his writings. Therefore, it is also imperative to discuss the standpoint of the author in relation to his own society and culture. Narayan belongs to the Malayarayar tribe and his novel *Kocharethi* provides a vivid account of the primal ways of life of the Adivasis and their shift towards citizenship in an independent India. In this novel, the writer is not trying to focus on the complex relationship between the Adivasi identity and a modern or a pro-modern consciousness. Instead, the writer wants to present his society as it is. Narayan (2011: xxvii) "prefers the role of one who observes and represents, rather than intervene directly". Therefore, he does not give any solutions nor does he elaborate the result of the policies followed by the colonial administrators or the government. Narayan believes that they (the Malayarayars) have their own distinctive way of life and their own value system. They are a strong, hardworking and self-sufficient community, and he wants to project the community as it is. This may be seen as a tendency to retain the traditional ways of life and also to document the fast disappearing ways of life. At the same time, such an act of self-representation can be understood as a resistance against the dominant structure of colonialism.

The very act of writing, for many ethnic writers, therefore, constitutes an act of 'writing back'. In this, the act of writing becomes a highly political act in which the marginalized and the underprivileged try to resist the dominant structures by adopting subversive means. In this chapter, we have seen how the use of folklore can constitute one of such subversive acts. Separated from the literary tradition which had always written about them without including them within it, these writers seek ways of reinventing their own traditions to carve out a separate tradition of their own. In this context, it would be worthwhile to ponder over the fact that Yeshe Dorjee Thongchi and Lummer Dai, though from Arunachal Pradesh, write in the long-established literary tradition of the Assamese language. As in the case of Narayan and many others, Thongchi and Dai belong to the group of ethnic writers who write in the language which was the medium of education for them. However, it would be foolhardy to assume that Thongchi, Dai and

Narayan subscribe to the same views regarding the literary traditions in which they have carved a niche for themselves.

Unlike Narayan, Thongchi, Dai or Rong Bong Terang do not write to avenge historical wrongs. Thongchi, for instance, has admitted in many interviews that he mainly started writing because of the inspiration and motivation he received from his Assamese teachers and friends. Having said this, the unconscious of a writer is a powerful motivating agent in shaping the structure of a literary work. Though Thongchi's fiction does not 'challenge' the 'dominant structures' in the manner that Narayan does, he does force the Assamese literary tradition to alter its own form to accommodate him as a writer with serious contributions, creating a new little tradition within it.

Writers around the world have experimented with the use of folkloric materials in their writings. The list of writers from Homer to Ovid to Shakespeare who have used folkloric elements in literature is in fact a very long one. However, this trend seems to have particularly found favour with contemporary women fiction writers starting from Margaret Atwood to Jeanette Winterson who have reworked ancient narratives for their fictional works. Ovid rendered the tragic myth of Philomela who communicated her tragic story by weaving her experience into an intricate cloth which her sister deciphers. One is here reminded of Christine Crow's *Miss X or the Wolf Woman* which is about the difficulties of expression in a traditional patriarchal world for both the female protagonist as well as the writer.

> The text encompasses many of the classical, biblical, literary and even psychoanalytic myths that have constituted Western culture, unravelling and representing these to demonstrate the ways they obliterate or falsely report women's experience. (Sellers, 2001: 52)

To conclude, folklore has a significant relationship with ethnicity. If ethnicity is understood in the manner of Cohen who "placed [a] greater emphasis on the ethnic group as a *collectively* organized strategy for the protection of economic and political interests" (Quoted in Jones, 1997: 74), it can be argued that folklore is one of the strategies for ethnic mobilization.

5

A Feminist Reading of *Kanyar Mulya* (Lummer Dai), *Alma Kabutari* (Maitreyi Pushpa), and Select Short Stories of Mahasweta Devi

In the Third World countries as well as in the minds of the Third World writers, the term 'feminism' carries very conflicting connotations, and the writers respond to it in very different ways. Barbara Fister in her book *Third World Women's Literature* (1995: 108) aptly remarks:

> Though many texts written by women in the third world are undeniably feminist in tone, their authors are frequently uncomfortable with that label. Buchi Emecheta, for example, calls herself a feminist with a small "f" in order to distance herself from the movement in the West.

If the feminist movement does not address itself also to the issues of race, class and imperialism, it cannot be relevant to alleviating the oppression of most of the women of the world (Johnson, 1991: 314–327). Feminism as a concept covers a range of views about injustice against women. It aims at defining, establishing and defending equal rights and opportunities for women. This struggle for equal rights and opportunities can be political, economic or social. The term 'feminism' is derived from the French term 'feminist' which was used regularly in English for a belief in and advocacy of equal rights for women based on the idea of the equality of the sexes. Milicent Fawcett, a leader of the suffragette movement in Britain, described the impact of feminism:

Other movements towards freedom have aimed at raising the status of a comparatively small group or class. But the women's movement aims at nothing less than raising the status of an entire sex—half the human race—to lift it up to the freedom and value of womanhood. It affects more people than any former reform movement, for it spreads over the whole world. It is more deep-seated, for it enters into the home and modifies the personal character. (quoted in Hannam, 2007: 1)

Feminist theory tries to understand the nature of gender inequality by examining women's social roles and their day-to-day experiences. Modern Western feminist movement is divided into three 'waves'. Each wave dealt with different aspects of the same feminist issues. The first wave feminism involved women's suffrage movements of the 19th and early 20th centuries. As a result, in 1920, the 19th amendment to the constitution of the United States of America guaranteed women the right to vote.

The ideas and actions of the women's liberation movements beginning in the late 1960s and early 1970s is termed as the second wave feminism. It campaigned for legal and social equality for women. In this wave, the feminists fought for greater equality across the section, in education, the workplace, and at home. Feminist writers have pointed to the difference between 'sex' and 'gender'. Feminist scholars believe that though a person's sex is predetermined and natural, one's gender is created by society. They view gender as a socially and culturally constructed category which is learned.

A tradition of feminist literary criticism may be said to have begun in the second wave of feminism. However, a fully formed feminist literary criticism did not suddenly emerge out of nowhere. The rise to prominence of feminist literary criticism in the second wave was a result of centuries "of women's writing, of women writing about women writing, and of women—and men—writing about women's minds, bodies, art and ideas" (Plain and Sellers, 2007: 2).

The third wave feminists like Judith Butler extended this argument to underline the fact that gender needs to be understood as a performance. Third wave feminism began in the 1990s as a more recent transformation of feminism. It is a continuation of, and a reaction to, the perceived failures of second wave feminism. The second wave feminists are often criticized by the third wave feminists for its lack of attention to the differences among men and women due to race, ethnicity, class, nationality, and emphasize 'identity' as a site of gender struggle. Actually, the second wave feminism coexists with the third wave feminism. Both the second and third wave feminists see women's cultural and political inequalities as inextricably linked and encourage women to understand aspects of their personal lives as deeply politicized and reflecting sexist power structures. Feminism has come a long way today from being a mere expression of dissatisfaction and protest against the material disadvantages faced by women to emerge as a philosophy that raises questions of positionality in the theories of Julia Kristeva. Kristeva believes that femaleness is a matter of choices, a choice between the semiotic of the mother and the symbolic of the father and not something intrinsic. Thus, feminism in literature, according to Kristeva, is a stance that one adopts, independent of whether the writer is a male or female. As Ruthven (1990: 99) says,

> From Kristeva's position, ... it would be somewhat naïve to conceive of the relationship between men and women as oppositional, for if women can be 'masculine' and men 'feminine' in negotiating the transaction between *le semiotique* ([S]emiotic) and the [S]ymbolic, there is no point in isolating 'women' as a special category on biological grounds and inventing something called feminism to protect their interests.

A similar idea emerges from a reading of Toril Moi's *Sexual/Textual Politics* (1988). Moi, a deconstructionist, problematizes the neat distinction between traditional masculine and feminine values. According to her, the very fact of being a female does not necessarily guarantee a feminist approach in literature. She tries to clarify the distinction between the often confused terms—feminist, feminine, and femaleness. Moi describes feminism as a political situation, femaleness as a matter of biology and femininity as a set of culturally defined characteristics (Moi, 1988: 65).

It is true that feminist movements and theoretical developments were led predominantly by middle-class white women from Western Europe and North America. Therefore, women of other countries have searched for alternative models of feminisms that would adequately reflect the socio-cultural realities of their own lives. In fact, women of developing countries and marginalized communities have proposed alternative or additional feminisms. As a result of this, the concept of 'womanism' emerged in African women's literature.

The very understanding of who is a feminist in the Indian context differs from that of the Western countries. It is significant that many Indian writers have rejected the 'feminist' label. Rather they would like to be called 'humanists'. In an interview with Gabrielle Collu, the Jnanpith award-winning Bengali writer Mahasweta Devi reacted to the interviewer's question regarding her stand as a feminist, she says, "I will not say feminist, but whenever I see woman, I want to bring out what they do" (Collu, 2008: 225). In the same interview she says, "I never consider myself as a woman writer, as a feminist" (Collu, 2008: 224). Similarly, the Jnanpith award-winning Assamese writer Mamoni Raisom Goswami refuses to be called a feminist crusader. She considers herself a humanist. Arupa Patangia Kalita, another woman writer of Assam, refused to accept Basanti Bordoloi Smriti Puraskar bestowed upon her by the Asom Sahitya Sabha in 1995 because she "believes that gender difference is irrelevant in the judgement of excellence in literary work" (from the blurb of her novel *Felani* [2003]).

Like other parts of the world, feminists in India seek gender equality: the right to work for equal wages, the right to equal access to health and education, and equal political rights. Historical circumstances and values in India have caused feminists to develop a feminism that differs from Western feminism. In 'Shashi Deshpande's *That Long Silence* (88): A Feminist Reading' (2004: 147), A.N. Dwivedi says,

> The Indian feminist movement has arisen in the form of a pointed protest against certain social customs, like *purdah system,* child marriage, dowry, polygamy, and *sati* (the practice of woman-burning on the husband's pyre).

Indian women negotiate survival through multiplicity of oppressive patriarchal family structures such as age, ordinal status, relationship to men through family of origin, marriage and procreation as well as patriarchal attributes. The heterogeneity of the Indian experience results in such multiple patriarchies, contributing to the existence of multiple feminisms. Hence, feminism in India is not a unidirectional, monolithic theoretical orientation; it is a pluralistic concept in India. Therefore, it has changed over time in relation to historical and cultural realities, levels of consciousness, perceptions and actions of individual women, and women as a group. Broadly speaking, feminism in India would be an awareness of women's oppression and exploitation in society, at work and within the family, and conscious action by women and men to change this situation (Bhasin and Khan, 1986).

When it comes to feminist perspective in ethnic fiction, it is imperative to deal with the representation of female characters in such fiction. However, any such attempt runs against certain stereotypes about ethnic communities in India that have a powerful hold on the people's imagination. For instance, it is generally believed that womenfolk in ethnic communities are less exploited and more privileged. Apparently, it seems that women in ethnic communities enjoy more freedom, and they have a powerful social identity. But the actual scenario might not be always so comforting.

In fact, women in ethnic communities are not really privileged. In contrast, they are doubly exploited in the sense that they belong to a group which is already 'marginalized'. Moreover, they are victims of sufferings and exploitations by virtue of being women. As such, they are more vulnerable to injustice, social oppression and violence. This emerges quite clearly in a study on the representation of female characters in ethnic novels.

Feminist literature refers to any literary work that focuses on the struggle of a woman for equality and the struggle to be accepted as a dignified human being, resisting repressive gender stereotypes. As such, feminist literature need not necessarily be the product of a female writer. Historically, there are many instances of male writers writing on women's issues, their troubles and their struggles for identity. Looking back, some of the champions of women's rights have been men—John Stuart Mill and Iswar Chandra Vidyasagar are examples of this. A name that figures prominently in the list of male writers who have taken up cudgels for women, envisioning a more just and equitable society is that of the Norwegian playwright Henrik Ibsen. Ibsen often focused on women, women issues and the troubles faced by them in a traditional patriarchal society. In his play *A Doll's House*, we observe a strong character in Nora Helmer who asserts her own beliefs and values to establish her own identity.

It would not be justifiable to claim that only those texts qualify as feminist ones that have a woman as the main protagonist. But it is important that characters in feminist literature resist the traditional role of women that is imposed by society. They want to make their own decisions, want to assert their beliefs and decisions and are ready to fight for their own identity as human beings.

A feminist reading of any text of literature would try to question the authority of the male as the supreme power, and feminist scholars seek to transform the patriarchal system of thought which posits the male as the norm. Feminists believe that existing inequalities between dominant and marginalized groups can and should be removed.

Elaine Showalter, in *A Literature of Their Own* (1977:13), discovers three major phases of historical development which she claims to be common to all literary movements. The first phase is known as the feminine phase. It refers to the initial stage of women's writing and it was mainly a stage of imitation (1840–1880). Second, there was a phase of protest against these standards that she calls the feminist phase (1880–1920). Finally, there is a phase of self-discovery which she calls the female phase (1920 onwards). She divides feminist criticism into two distinct varieties. The first is *feminist critique* concerned with woman as the consumer of male-produced literature. Its main concerns are the images and stereotypes of women in literature, the omissions and the misconceptions about women in criticism, and the fissures in male-constructed literary history. *Gynocritics* is concerned with woman as the producer of textual meaning. Though the *feminist critique* is essentially political and polemical, *gynocritics* is more self-contained and experimental. I undertake a feminist critique of ethnic fiction, but in doing this I have slightly qualified the sense in which Showalter uses the term. I intend to look at not just the images and stereotypes in literature, but also the acts of resistance.

I would like to begin with a discussion of Lummer Dai's novel *Kanyar Mulya* (The Bride Price) for which he received the Sitanath Brahma Choudhury award from the Asom Sahitya Sabha. The award is for the best novel written in Assamese language by the writers of any ethnic community whose mother tongue is not Assamese. The novel depicts the Adi social life through the presentation of one of the social institutions of marriage. The protagonist Gumba is the victim of the long-established tradition of the Adis—that is the social practice of giving and taking bride price. This particular theme of the novel easily lends the novel to a feminist interpretation. The very nature of the theme highlights the commodification of woman; a woman can be sold and bought in the Adi society as in the Adi society a girl's marriage is fixed at an early age, even when she is in the womb of her mother. The marriage is sometimes fixed just after birth, taking the price of the bride from the groom's family. The first sentence of the novel—*I sold the girl a few years back*—definitely helps to create the idea of the commodification of woman. She was sold to Dakat, and for this, her father earned five mithuns, seven cows, eleven dishes and six brass bowls.

It would be appropriate to quote Michael Ryan (2002: 101) in this context, who says:

> According to the feminist theory, the subordination of women originated in primitive societies in which women served as objects of exchange between father-dominated families that formed alliances through marriage. While such clan relations have been replaced in contemporary capitalist societies by more fluid forms of sexual alliance, the modern industrial world is still by and large patriarchal in character.

But the significant point here is that we do sense a voice of protest against such male domination and traditional patriarchal values all through the novel. The protagonist Gumba voices her strong feelings against social practices like child marriage and bride price before she comes to know about her own marriage. When she learns about her marriage, she protests:

> Kill me father. Do kill me. It would be better to kill than to sell me. (Dai, 2004: 9; my translation)

When she is forcibly taken from school to her in laws' place by Mindak and his relatives, she puts up a brave front against the old practice:

> The days are gone when you could sell and buy human beings. Today there is no girl who will allow herself to be sold and bought like mithuns and cows. (Dai, 2004: 37; my translation)

That is not the end of her bold protest against commodification of girls by the traditional society. She does not give up her protest even when she is forcefully locked up in Mindak's house. In fact, she is determined not to surrender till death. She refuses to eat anything for sixteen days when she is forcefully kept in Mindak's house (Dai, 2004: 67).

Feminism is manifested in the novel in the form of a protest against the established patriarchal norms and the attempt to establish one's own identity. In fact, the entire novel is about Gumba's physical and mental torture and her strong protest against it. There are many characters in the novel who talk of woman as commodity. Tumde, an advocate of male domination and patriarchy, says to Gumba in the *kebang*:

> We have bought you. So we need not argue with you about anything. We can do whatever we want with you. After all, who would bother to argue with a purchased commodity? (Dai, 2004: 91; my translation)

Similarly, Borgam Itum says:

> Even if Gumba prefers to die without having anything in Mindak's house, no one should worry. As Mindak has bought her, he has complete right over her. After taking the price for her, Kargum, her father, does not have right to say anything. (Dai, 2004: 98; my translation)

Here Gumba is seen as a commodity—a cow or a mithun—which once bought, is the sole property of the owner.

The feminist zeal of the novelist manifests itself in the protest against male domination. Gumba's protest against the long-established system of child marriage is a protest against patriarchy. Feminism is manifest in the novel in the protagonist's protest against a repressive patriarchal custom and the attempt to assert her identity. Gumba's protest is best reflected in her sixteen days' long fast in Mindak's house. In response to a statement by the Borgam who says that she has decided to die than to marry Dakat, she says,

> No, I didn't decide that it is better to die than live. I did have desire to live, even now I wish to live. But Mindak's house is like a house of death where I could not eat anything. (Dai, 2004: 90; my translation)

It is not only Gumba who protests against male domination and exploitation. Gumba's marriage (child-marriage) is protested by her school friends. An educated youth, Minjum, too speaks against the traditional patriarchal values of the society. The chorus and the play that are presented in the cultural function in the presence of the Deputy Commissioner speak against the custom of child-marriage and bride-price in Adi society. The banners and placards in the hands of the students contain slogans such as:

It is a sin to sell the daughter.

Do away with child marriage.

To take price for your daughter is to drink your own blood.

Treat women humanely. (Dai, 2004: 46)

These slogans and the procession in favour of Gumba's release definitely hint at a strong sense of feminist consciousness.

Though Mahasweta Devi never considers herself as a woman writer or as a feminist (Sen and Yadav, 2008: 224), her fiction easily lends itself to a feminist interpretation. Malini Bhattacharya (1997: 1004) says that "Mahasweta Devi has never described herself as a feminist. This is because in her perception sexual exploitation always forms part of a much larger pattern of exploitation." Mahasweta Devi's fiction needs to be seen against the backdrop of the rise of a new crop of writers who "are rushing in to occupy a newly appointed public 'feminist' space" (Shahani and Ghosh, 2000: 3814). These novelists mainly write about the "formulaic expressions of domestic oppression, personal angst, inter-generational inspiration, or intra-generational bonding among women that seem to peel off from any larger historical attachment" (Shahani and Ghosh, 2000: 3814).

But many of her stories are women-centred with the gender issue offering an exemplum of other issues. Her works mostly deal with the unprivileged tribal women and the atrocities inflicted on them. Feminist scholars see her powerful tales of exploitation and struggle as extremely rich sites of feminist discourse. I will focus on three of her long stories which have also been sometimes labelled as novellas.

These three stories are 'Doulati', 'Palamo' and 'Gauhan'. Moreover, two other stories, 'Draupadi' and 'Bayen', will also be analysed in the light of feminism. In all of these stories, Devi's protagonist is a woman belonging to an ethnic community. The woman protagonist of 'Doulati' belongs to the Nagesia tribe while the protagonist of 'Palamo' and 'Gauhan' belong to the Bhuiyan tribe. In 'Draupadi', the female protagonist is a member of the Santhal tribe, and in 'Bayen', she belongs to the Dome tribe.

In the story 'Draupadi', Draupadi (Dropdi Mehjen) is a twenty-seven-year-old widow. She is a wanted woman in 'Operation Forest Jharkhand'. The mission of the armed forces is to execute her along with her husband Dulna who are responsible for the murder and mayhem of their oppressors. The politically active Dropdi had a hand in the killings of a few atrocious landlords. Finally apprehended by the army, Dropdi is tortured and raped. The morning after her rape, she refuses to clothe and wash herself. In refusing to obey the command of the Senanayak, the army commander, she appears to be a very strong lady. The last sentence of the story very well sums up the character's strength and bold protest against the male dominance and patriarchal order:

> Draupadi pushes Senanayak with her two mangled breasts and for the first time Senanayak is afraid to stand before an unarmed *target*, terribly afraid. (Devi, 1997d: 37)

Rajeshwari Sunder Rajan says, "It is simultaneously a deliberate refusal of a shared sign-system [pertaining to nakedness and rape] and an ironic deployment of the same semiotics to create the disconcerting counter effects of shame, confusion and terror in the enemy." And male sexual violence is defeated simply by its demystification and Dropdi emerges as a "terrifying super object—an unarmed target" (quoted in Devi, 1997d: 244).

Savita Goel (1999: 207) sees Dropdi's ways of protest as very different, making it an extremely shocking, powerful and innovative narrative. It is interesting to note that the military authorities are confused about her real name, Dropdi or Draupadi. Dropdi is a simple tribal name, and Draupadi is derived from the name of the famous character in *Mahabharata*. We observe a significant departure in the treatment of the character of Draupadi in these two texts. In the epic, Draupadi is treated as an object and is used to demonstrate male power and glory. When her husband (Judhisthira) puts her on stake in a game of dice, she does not protest. The Kauravas try to outrage her modesty by pulling off the sari that she wears. But, in Mahasweta Devi's story, Dropdi is not a passive character. Here, Dropdi raises her voice against extreme torture and atrocity. The feminist consciousness of the author (though she refuses to be labelled so) does not allow the female protagonist to be a passive recipient of the ill-treatment meted out to her.

When Dropdi is captured by the Indian forces and cross-interrogated for an hour, she does not utter a word. The Senanayak commands the soldiers, "Make her. Do the needful" (Devi, 1997d: 34). Dropdi is sexually harassed; throughout the long night she is raped and mutilated by countless lustful men. Next morning, she walks naked towards Senanayak in bright sunlight and says:

> ...what's the use of clothes? You can strip me, but how can you clothe me again? ...there isn't a man here that I should be ashamed. (Devi, 1997d: 36)

In this story by Devi, the protagonist is not saved by any male, but in her own way, she protests against the patriarchal structure and exploitation of women. According to Savita Goel (1999: 208), Devi "stresses on the materiality of what women are for men; literally a 'target' on which they can exercise their power" and she adds:

> Draupadi acquires a new self-definition and becomes the active maker of her own meaning. She refuses to remain an object [in Mahasweta Devi's story] of a male narrative, asserts herself as 'subject' and emphasizes on the truth of her own presence.

In the introduction of the translation of the stories by Mahasweta Devi, Gayatri Chakravorty Spivak says, "Dropdi is (as heroic as) Draupadi. She is also what Draupadi—written into the patriarchal and authoritative sacred text as proof of male power—could not be. (Devi, 1997d: 11)

The story 'Bayen', based on a superstition, focuses on a tribal woman named Chandi. Society brands her as *bayen* (witch) and excommunicates her. It is believed that if the *bayen* comes across a child or a youth, she sucks his/her blood. The story looks at Chandi's life and analyzes how she came to be branded as a *bayen*. Once Chandi's sister-in-law's daughter had small pox and she took her to the temple of Sheetla Mata and prayed for her well-being but the child died. Everyone blamed Chandi for her death and called her a witch (*bayen*). She is hurt and shocked and decides to give up her ancestral job of burying dead children. She is branded as *bayen*, as people in the village believe that she suckled the dead children. While performing the death rituals of the child of her sister-in-law, she thinks of her own son Bhagirath and she sings a lullaby. The village crowd, which was observing her, shouts, "You are a *bayen*" (Devi, 1995: 114). In answer to that, Chandi says, "I am not a *bayen*. Milk oozes from my breast. But I am not a *bayen*. Why don't you clarify, Gangaputtra, that I am not a *bayen*?" (Devi, 1995: 114). But Chandi's husband too declares that she is a *bayen*. Thus, the story unravels the trials of a woman who bears the brunt of a widespread superstition.

Sceptics might argue that at one level there is nothing feminist about it; while it is indeed a story about suppression and exploitation of women, they might argue that it does not question the position of women in this society nor does it raise any protest against such exploitation. However, this would be too simplistic a reading of a story that is deeply embedded in the ethos of Chandi's society. Though Chandi is excommunicated by her society, death gives her acceptance. She establishes her position in the society not in her life, but by her death.

She sees some people piling bamboo poles on the railway track to obstruct and stop the train, so that they can attack and loot it. When she sees the approaching train, she raises her lantern and screams for the train to stop. As she stands before the pile of bamboo poles to prevent the disaster, she is crushed under its wheels. She is awarded posthumously by the government of India for her bravery. Chandi sacrificed her life to save the train from accident. The BDO came to Malinder (Chandi husband)'s village and said that she had done something extremely bold. Chandi's son declared himself as Chandi's offspring and accepted the award given to her. Through this sacrifice, she proves her courage and also proves her concern for the society which has excommunicated her. Her identity as a genuine member of the society is established at last. Through this narrative, Mahasweta Devi tries to establish that woman does possess inner strength and the existence of each and every woman is meaningful in one way or the other. The emphasis on woman's strength and existence allows Devi to highlight feminist consciousness. In the essay 'Tribal Women in the Selected Works of Mahasweta Devi' (1999: 210), Savita Goel says,

> Mahasweta Devi contends that women should not be passive and submissive and should realize the inner strength which they possess. They should be aware that their own existence is meaningful, that their suffering is imposed and have firm conviction in their own potential to reshape their lives.

Mahasweta Devi's stories 'Doulati' and 'Palomo' deal with the theme of bonded labour and prostitution. While Doulati, a fourteen-year-old girl, is entrapped by a man from a high class who, after promising to marry her, leaves her in a brothel; Basmati, the protagonist of 'Palamo' is compelled to become a prostitute by her husband. 'Doulati' focuses on the extreme form of violence against women, her economic and sexual exploitation, trade (commodification) of women as well as the physical and mental trauma faced by the prostitutes.

In 'Doulati', Devi portrays the pathetic lives of the prostitutes and the agony of rejected prostitutes and their anonymous death. Doulati is shocked to see that when the prostitutes can no longer attract men and satisfy their lust, they are thrown out to become beggars or to die on the streets. Devi's description of the lives of the prostitutes speaks volumes of her concern for them:

> The social system that makes Crook Nagesia a kamiya is made by men. Therefore do Doulati, Somni, Reoti have to quench the hunger of male flesh. (Devi, 2001a: 62)

In a discussion of Mahasweta Devi's 'Doulati', Gabrielle Collu (1999: 49) says:

> Tribal women are oppressed on several levels. First, because they are women in a patriarchal and patrilineal society. Although in most tribal societies in India, women's position is relatively better than in Hindu caste society,

property is still transmitted through the male line, and in general women do not have access to political power.

Collu mentions that tribal women are oppressed because they belong to a group considered inferior because of their ethnic or caste position. Moreover, they are oppressed because as women they are used and controlled by those who have the power to oppress their people. She adds:

> Rape, torture and forced prostitution are the means landowners and police employ to humiliate, punish and establish control over an entire community which is economically and materially dependent. (1999: 49)

Though Doulati resigns herself to her fate and dies a miserable plight, the novella powerfully depicts the violence inflicted on helpless women and the ruthlessness of men.

It is important to note that Mahasweta Devi's 'Doulati' is an allegory of the nation-state of India. The story ends in 1975, just as Indira Gandhi's declares Emergency throughout the country. Doulati is a bonded-sex-worker who is 27 years old and is used, exploited, plundered, wasted and abandoned. She walks to the village of Bahri where Mohan Srivastava is preparing for the celebration of Independence Day by drawing a huge map of India in the courtyard. It is interesting that Doulati throws up blood and dies on that map:

> Filling the entire Indian peninsula from the oceans to the Himalayas, here lies *bonded labour* spread-eagled, kamiya-whore Doulati Nagesia's tormented corpse, putrefied with vulnerable disease, having vomited up all the blood in its desiccated lungs. Today, on the fifteenth of *August*, Doulati has left no room at all in the India of people like Mohan for planting the standard of the Independence flag. What will Mohan do now? Doulati is all over India. (Devi, 2001a: 94)

According to Gabrielle Collu (1999: 55), this passage shows that Independence is a lie, a meaningless issue for the majority of Indians. She says:

> This passage suggests the complete identification of the exploited *Adivasi* woman with India: she is all over India; she is India—meaning that the

poor, exploited workers compose the majority of the people of India and that Independence is a lie for the vast majority of people in India or at the very least that it is meaningless to them.

Devi's use of the image of the bonded-sex-worker lying dead on a map of India can be seen as condemnation of exploitation and crushing of the myth of a free India. Collu (1999: 55) then adds, "She [Mahasweta] suggests that real independence is impossible as long as there is gender, social and material inequality enabling one group to abuse another."

In view of this, it is insignificant whether the protagonist in 'Doulati' is a bold woman who can protest against the exploitation and torture meted out to them. Doulati herself might be a very passive character who can never raise her voice against any kind of exploitation, but the novella itself is a strong voice against all kinds of inequality prevailing in the society.

In the story 'Palamo', Mahasweta Devi deals with the theme of prostitution and focuses on the problem of child-marriage. Here, the protagonist Basmati is compelled by her husband to become a prostitute. Moreover, she is a victim of child-marriage. She is married to Nanku at the age of seven. Basmati is portrayed as a very strong character who dares not only to protest but to take up action against men who subject women to harassment. When a high-caste man sexually harasses her in the field, she picks up a knife and cuts off his hand, without pondering over the consequences. Madho appreciates her courage and says:

> You have showed a lot of courage. If all women possess this much courage, then the abuse of tribal women would not happen. (Devi, 1997c: 123–124; my translation)

Even when she is put into the brothel, she tries to find out strategies to escape from there and finally succeeds and reaches her village.

In the novella, 'Gauhan', the writer expresses the self-assertive nature of a tribal woman, Jhalo, through the symbol of *gauhan* which means a 'venomous snake'. Jhalo protests every time she is subjected to torture or harassment. When her husband died in a coal mine accident, she was asked to work without pay. But she refused and said, "I have neither put my thumb impression nor borrowed money, why should I do unpaid labour" (Devi, 1997b: 183). She is told by her brother-in-law that Government has passed a law to abolish the tradition of bonded labour. She wonders why no one protests against injustice.

This novella has a number of incidents which describe the violence committed against women. Moni is such a character who (when she is in her youth) refuses to be a bonded labourer saying that the custom of bonded labourer has been abolished. But she is struck with a red hot iron rod for her defiance. Jhalo is very assertive and bold. When the Tehsildar wants to sexually abuse her, she shouts and bites his hand like a tiger making him cry out in pain. She does not consider it her destiny to endure the cruelty and torture of the upper class people. Instead she protests against all such cases of violence and exploitation meted out against women. She complains to Amin Babu for whom the Tehsildar works: "How dare you people of high class treat us like prostitutes?" (Devi, 1997b: 184). When Amin Babu consoles her and says that such things would not happen in the future and that she is like his mother, sister and daughter, she says:

> Will you give the same kind of punishment to the Tehsildar now that you would have given, if your mother, sister or daughter would have been humiliated in the same manner? (Devi, 1997b: 184)

This is solid argument coming from the least expected source—a woman belonging to a tribe. It would have been 'normal' and 'natural' (at least till than) for such a woman to accept whatever was decided for her by others. Jhalo's arguments definitely establish her position as a woman who can fight for her honour, her identity. As a result, Amin Babu announces, "Mother, what you have done to protect your honour will be published in the newspapers, the government will give you awards.... These people tried to taint your honour but you bit them like a poisonous snake, 'gauhan'" (Devi, 1997b: 185). In Savita Goel's words (1999: 206), "This act of Gauhan infuses a spirit of confidence and courage in the otherwise passive tribals. For the first time they said that if their women were dishonoured they would not let anyone rest in peace."

In many ways, Maitreyi Pushpa's writings have made a significant role in the tradition of women's writing in Hindi. Unlike Mahasweta Devi, she strongly challenges the notion that literature is never male or female. According to Anita Vashista (2006), "[b]oth through her occasional public utterances and statements as well as through her creative work, [Pushpa] has struggled steadily to emphasise the difference between the status and standpoint of women and men." In an article entitled 'Nayika se Muthbhed' (A Confrontation with the Heroine), the artist, she asserts, is not "a mere craftsperson fabricating lifeless figures on a potter's wheel, but a woman or a man with a distinct gender bias and perspective, creating characters who are painfully living and breathing, demanding justice and fair representation" (quoted in Vashista, 2006). In fact, Pushpa has questioned the competence of men to represent the battered female psyche, its conflicts and needs. In her assessment, man portraying the predominantly deprived and exploited life-story of the Indian woman is akin to a male character (quoted in Vashista, 2006).

Showalter (1979: 27) has said that it is not enough for feminist criticism to limit itself to the male-created "stereotypes of women, the sexism of male critics, and the limited roles women play in literary history, we are not learning what women have felt and experienced, but only what men have thought women should be." In *Alma Kabutari*, Maitreyi Pushpa tackles the old kabutara tradition of sexual slavery of the Kajja tribe and its impact on the lives of women. The onus of reclaiming a dignified status for her oppressed people falls on the young shoulders of Alma. In depicting this, Pushpa redefines the contours of traditional female heroism in the context of contemporary Indian fiction. Alma suffers to survive and then takes on the repressive social practices that has for long pushed her people to the margins. Labelled as a criminal tribe during the British regime, the kabutaras have been subjected to social, economical and sexual exploitation by the upper castes in a dehumanizing feudal setup.

> It was said that when the British started hounding the fellow fighters of the Rani of Jhansi after she fell in battle, they spread wherever they could, like water.... Those that were soaked in by the soil and earth of Bundelkhand were people whose language, lifestyle and customs were like those of the

people of that soil. But those that couldn't pass this test? Strange of language and dress, this lot stood out from the rest and easily got targeted. (Pushpa, 2006: 16)

Poor and landless, the kabutaras have been completely shunned by society at large and they live in the margins of 'civilized' life. Sumit Guha, in his *Environment and Ethnicity in India, 1200–1991* (1999: 56), describes:

> It is evident ... that the forest dwellers are seen as kind of necessary evil, impossible to extirpate but to be turned to advantage whenever possible. Their habitat is to be destroyed in the interior of the kingdom, but encouraged on its borders as a defensive bulwark.

Thus, much to the pleasant surprise of the landholding farmers, the small group of kabutaras who first came to the outskirts of Madora Khurd were more than happy to serve for free just for a plot of land to stay in:

> How were they to know that the kabutaras had found port here after heavy and fatal battering to their pride? That humiliation has gone deep into their souls? That now they wanted to befriend anyone at any cost? That this had now become their goal of life? (Pushpa, 2006: 16)

Education gives Alma a sense of empowerment which allows her to create an identity for herself. Like Mahasweta Devi's Dropdi, when paraded naked in front of Shriram Shastri, Alma does not make any attempt to hide her nakedness. Her naked body unnerves Shriram Shastri:

> He was familiar with the stubbornness of woman, the kind of woman that kept the cloak of shame and modesty wrapped tight around her, on guard, resistant. But this girl was not keen on even the pretence of a purdah! Her openness unnerved Shriram. (Pushpa, 2006: 554)

At the climax of the novel, Alma becomes an embodiment of woman's dignity, successfully resisting and challenging male domination and repressive practices. Much to the chagrin of the upper caste, Alma sets fire to the sandalwood pyre of Shriram Shastri.

As if under a spell, the vast concourse of people sees Alma emerge from the
black folds of the smoke like the Goddess Durga and descend the steps of
the platform of the pyre. (Pushpa, 2006: 599)

To conclude, it has often been said that the American white feminist criticism has not paid attention to the intricate ways in which issues of gender are tied up with issues of class, race and caste. British Marxist feminist critics have discussed the interpolation of class and gender. A reading of the select Indian fiction that has been undertaken in this chapter most certainly points to the ways in which gender issues in the Indian context cannot be dealt with in isolation. As Chandra Talpade Mohanty (1991) argues that assumptions of privilege and ethnocentric universality on the one hand, and inadequate self-consciousness about the effect of Western scholarship on the 'Third World' in the context of a world system dominated by the West on the other, characterize a sizable extent of Western feminist work on women in the Third World. Any discussion of the intellectual and political construction of 'Third World feminisms' must address itself to two simultaneous projects: the internal critique of hegemonic 'Western' feminisms, and the formulation of autonomous, geographically, historically, and culturally grounded feminist concerns and strategies; unless these two tasks are addressed simultaneously, 'Third World' feminisms run the risk of marginalization or ghettoization from both mainstream (Left and Right) and Western feminist discourses (Mohanty, 1991: 51).

Feminism interrogates the patriarchal structure of society, and it opposes women's subordination to men in public and private spheres of life. If Third World feminists have not entirely lost faith in the 'Western' idea of emancipation, with all that it promises—self-determination and personal autonomy, equality in the public and private sphere— one has to combat all relations of patriarchy, Western and ancestral (Nanda, 1996: WS2). Yet, ancestral oppressions do not become any less cruel just because they are 'our own', and alien ideas do not exhaust themselves just because they are 'not ours'. This reasoning obviously represents the worst kind of genetic fallacy and can only lead to a suffocating, reactionary nationalism which has never been anything but oppressive for women (Nanda, 1996: WS2). Ethnic nationalism has very often led to the violation of human rights in many parts of the world. Claims for ethnic homelands, for instance, are very often based on an exclusivist agenda and a primitive understanding of difference and superiority. Thus abuse of human rights is common in areas where there is a conflict of interest among competing ethnic groups.

Irrespective of the evident discomfort of some Indian women writers with the 'feminist' label, it is amply clear that women in the Indian context are doubly marginalized. Ironically, many of the women characters that we have looked at in this chapter belong to communities that are in any case marginalized. One also needs to contest the oft-stated view that India is a land where women are worshipped as goddesses. It needs to be seen that "the respect and privileges which accompany the position of a '*devi*' (Goddess) are not only anti-individualistic", but they also "deny women a personhood" (Jain and Singh, 2001: 10). At the other extreme of our society, women are just treated as sexual objects or things of exchange, again denying their humanity, their wishes and desires, their individual self.

6

Conclusion

That fiction is a powerful vehicle of self-expression and social criticism for writers is undeniable. Fiction is always attached to life. This seems particularly true in the context of ethnographic fiction or fiction depicting ethnic life and societies. But it is also true that fiction permits a degree of freedom and autonomy that is granted to writers by virtue of the fact that fiction wears the garb of presenting imaginative truth. However, considering the fact that we are living in an age when the idea of truth itself has come under the scanner, what is the nature of truth that is conveyed through fiction? And what is the border between ethnography and fiction?

In 'Ethnography and Fiction: Where Is the Border?' (1999), Kirin Narayan identifies four points of divergence. First, where ethnography tries to clarify issues, fiction withholds information. Second, ethnography, as against fiction, relies more explicitly on generalizations. Third, traditionally, ethnography strives to achieve the native's point of view, but in fiction writers have no qualms about shifting between different subjective worlds, thought processes, and emotions of their characters. Last, the most important difference between fiction and ethnography lies in the question of accountability:

> Even though sophisticated readers may be aware that fiction is a potent medium for emotional facts and symbolic truths, it is understood that characters need not actually exist and episodes need not actually happen. Explicitly locating a work within a genre, then, becomes crucial to how it is received. (Narayan, 1999: 142)

Narayan, of course, qualifies each of these differences, taking care to show how very often there can be a 'transgression' of disciplinary boundaries. Nevertheless, I believe that the third and fourth points of divergence between fiction and ethnography relating to accountability and subjectivity need further elaboration from the point of view of this book. How much freedom can a fiction writer exercise when it comes to literary representation? Talking about North America, Arnold Krupat (1992: 21) writes:

> One may grant that not all Euramericans were rapacious, genocidal monsters, and that not all Indians were, in the purest and most absolute sense, their hapless, innocent victims: nonetheless, it seems to me beyond question that—all things considered—the indigenous peoples of this continent, along with African Americans, women, and many other groups, have overwhelmingly been more sinned against than sinning. If this is so, to construct one's discourse on such a premise is not necessarily to engage in the revisionist allegory of victimism. Some people *have* been hurt by others and if that is not the only and the most interesting thing to say, it most certainly remains something that still, today, can probably not be said too often.

This argument is perfectly valid in the context of a multiethnic society such as India where the tribes have been relegated to the margins of civilized society. Mahasweta Devi, author and activist, mentions:

> The tribals and the mainstream have always been parallel. There has never been a meeting point.... They do not understand mainstream machination, so although there are safeguarding laws against land-grabbing, tribal land is being sold illegally every day, and usurped by mainstream society all over India, especially in West Bengal. (Devi, 2001a: ii–iii)

Colonial discourse helped to generate the idea of the inferiority of the colonial subject and to exercise hegemonic control over them through control of the dominant modes of public and private representation. Drawing on the critiques of language by poststructuralist thinkers such as Jacques Derrida, Jacques Lacan, and Michel Foucault, postcolonialism contend that essentialist cultural categories are flawed. On the other hand,

[...] theorists warned of the dangers of simply reversing the categories of oppressed and oppressor without critiquing the process by which such simple binaries had come into being in the first place. They also warned of the dangers of creating a new indigenous élite who would act merely as neocolonial puppets for the old forces of the colonizing powers. (Ashcroft, Griffiths, Tiffin, 1998: 78)

Gayatri Spivak has pointed to the danger of allowing the subaltern forces to speak, without recognizing that their essential subjectivity has been and still is shaped by the discourses by which they were constructed as subaltern. Her controversial question 'Can the Subaltern Speak?' was frequently misinterpreted to mean that there was no way in which subalterns could ever attain a voice. In actual fact,

> Spivak's essay is not an assertion of the inability of the subaltern voice to be accessed or given agency, but only a warning to avoid the idea that the subaltern can ever be isolated in some absolute, essentialist way from the play of discourses and institutional practices that give it its voice. (Ashcroft, Griffiths, Tiffin, 1998: 79)

Talking about the failure of Western feminism to take into account the experiences of Third World women, Spivak asserts that "varieties of feminist criticism and practice must reckon with the possibility that, like any other discursive practice, they are marked and constituted by, even as they constitute, the field of their production" (Morton, 2003: 40). Western feminism repeats the universalist errors of masculine-centred truth claims or objective knowledge by suggesting that all women the world over suffer from the same sort of oppression simply because they are women. Against this 'lie' of 'global sisterhood', Spivak has thus criticized western feminism for ignoring the plight of 'Third World' women (Morton, 2003: 40). I think that we must guard against similar pitfalls in Comparative Literature. A search for 'literary universals' should not lead to another lie of 'global tribalhood'. Nor do I intend to study Indian realities in terms of the literary representation of Indian tribe, the shortcomings of such an approach being already pointed out by Ngugi wa Thiong'o in *Decolonising the Mind* (1987) in the context of African literature.

However, I do believe that an awareness of this warning would go a long way in giving expression to the repressed voices in the margins. Writers, both of fiction and of ethnography, thus have to address questions of accountability. And in doing this, the fiction writer has to be aware that writing from within may not be as uncomplicated an issue as it has sometimes been assumed. As I have tried to show in this book, the idea of the writer inhabiting a unique cultural space that is 'untouched' and 'uncorrupted' by outside influence needs to be questioned.

Bibliography

English

Ahmad, Aijaz. 1994. *In Theory: Classes, Nations, Literatures*. Delhi: Oxford University Press.
———. 2004. *On Communalism and Globalization: Offensives of the Far Right*. New Delhi: Three Essays Collective.
Anderson, Benedict. 2006. *Imagined Communities: Reflections on the Origin and Spread of Nationalism*. London: Verso.
Ashcroft, Bill, Gareth Griffiths and Helen Tiffin. 1998. *Key Concepts in Post-Colonial Studies*. New York: Routledge.
———. 2002. *The Empire Writes Back: Theory and Practice in Post-Colonial Literatures*. New York and London: Routledge.
Barber, K. 1999. 'Pakeha Ethnicity and Indigeneity', *Social Analysis: The International Journal of Social and Cultural Practice,* 43 (2): 33–40. URL: http://www.jstor.org/stable/23166519 (accessed on 20.05.2012).
Bardhan, Kalpana. 1990. *Of Women, Outcasts, Peasants and Rebels*. Berkeley: University of California Press.
Barker, Chris. 2004. *The SAGE Dictionary of Cultural Studies*. London and New Delhi: SAGE.
Barth, Fredrik. (ed.). 1969. *Ethnic Groups and Boundaries*. Long Grove, Illinois: Waveland Press.
Barthes, Roland. 2001. 'The Death of the Author', in Vincent B. Leitch (ed.), *The Norton Anthology of Theory and Criticism*. New York: Norton, pp. 1466–1470.
Baruah, Sanjib. 2001. *India against Itself: Assam and the Politics of Identity*. New Delhi: Oxford University Press.
———. 2008. 'Territoriality, Indigeneity and Rights in the North-east India', *Economic and Political Weekly*, XLIII (12–13): 15–19.
Bates, R.H. 1974. 'Ethnic Competition and Modernization in Contemporary Africa', *Comparative Political Studies*, 6 (4): 457–484.
Baviskar, Amita. 2005. 'Indian Indigeneities: Adivasi Engagements with Hindu Nationalism in India', paper presented in the conference on 'Indigenous Experience Today', Wenner-Gren Foundation, 19–24 March, pp. 1–30.

Bennett, Paul L. 1952. 'Folklore and the Literature to Come', *The Journal of American Folklore*, American Folklore Society, 65 (255): 23–27. URL: http://www.jstor.org/stable/536284 (accessed on 26.06.2013).

Bernheimer, Charles (ed.). 1995. *Comparative Literature in the Age of Multiculturalism*. Baltimore and London: The Johns Hopkins University Press.

Bertens, Hans. 2008. *Literary Theory: The Basics*. London and New York: Routledge.

Beteille, Andre. 1991. 'The Concept of Tribe, With Special Reference to India', in A. Beteille, *Society and Politics in India: Essays in a Comparative Sociology*, London, pp. 57–78.

———. 1998. 'The Idea of Indigenous People', *Current Anthropology*, 39 (2): 187–192.

———. 1999. *Society and Politics in India: Essays in a Comparative Perspective*. Oxford: Oxford University Press.

Bhasin, Kamala and Nighat Said Khan. 1986. *Some Questions on Feminism and Its Relevance in South Asia*. New Delhi: Kali for Women.

Bhattacharya, Malini. 1997. 'Mahasweta Devi: Activist and Writer', *Economic and Political Weekly*, 32 (19): 1003–1004.

Biswas, Prasenjit and Chandan Suklabaidya. 2008. *Ethnic Life-Worlds in North-East India: An Analysis*. New Delhi: SAGE India.

Borang, Kaling. 2006. 'My Pyaayi: The Feather on the Hat', *Silifor Review*, 2 (II): 2–8.

Bullock, Marcus. 1979. 'The Enclosure of Consciousness: Theory of Representation in Literature', *Comparative Literature*, 94 (5): 931–955. URL: http://www.jstor.org/stable/2906561 (accessed on 01.07.2013).

Chakladar, Arnab. 2011. 'Language, Nation and the Question of "Indian Literature"', *Postcolonial Text*, 6 (4): 1–15.

Chakravarty, Saumita. (ed.). 2007. *Three Sides of Life: Short Stories by Bengali Women Writers*. New Delhi: Oxford University Press.

Chaturvedi, A.K. 2008. *Tribals in Indian English Novel*. New Delhi: Atlantic Publishers and Distributors.

Chowdhury, J.N. 1983. *Arunachal Pradesh: From Frontier Tracts to Union Territory*. New Delhi: Cosmo Publications.

Clifford, James. 1986a. 'Introduction: Partial Truths', in James Clifford and George E. Marcus (eds), *Writing Culture: The Poetics and Politics of Ethnography*. Berkeley: University of California Press, pp. 1–26.

———. 1986b. 'On Ethnographic Allegory', in James Clifford and George E. Marcus (eds), *Writing Culture: The Poetics and Politics of Ethnography*. Berkeley: University of California Press, pp. 98–121.

Cohen, Ronald. 1978. 'Ethnicity: Problem and Focus in Anthropology', *Annual Review of Anthropology*, 7: 379–403.

Collu, Gabrielle. 1999. 'Adivasis and the Myth of Independence: Mahasweta Devi's "Doulati the Bountiful"', *A Review of International English Literature*, 30 (1): 43–57.

Collu, Gabrielle. 2008. 'Speaking with Mahasweta Devi: Mahasweta Devi interviewed by Gabrielle Collu', in Nivedita Sen and Nikhil Yadav (eds), *Mahasweta Devi: An Anthology of Recent Criticism*. New Delhi: Pencraft International, pp. 221–228.

Cowen, M. and R. Shenton. 1995. 'The Invention of Development', in J. Crush (ed.), *Power of Development*. London: Routledge, pp. 27–43.

Das, Nigamananda (ed.). 2011. *Matrix of Redemption: Contemporary Multi-Ethnic English Literature from North East India*. New Delhi: Adhyayan Publishers and Distributors.

Das, Sisir Kumar. 2011. 'Comparative Literature in India: A Historical Perspective', *Sahitya*: Journal of the Comparative Literature Association of India, no. 1: 18–30.

Dev, Amiya. 1984. *The Idea of Comparative Literature in India*. Calcutta: Papyrus.

———. 2000. 'Comparative Literature in India', *Comparative Literature and Culture*, 2 (4): 1–8.

Dev, Amiya and Sisir Kumar Das (eds). 1989. *Comparative Literature: Theory and Practice*. Simla: Indian Institute of Advanced Study.

Dev, Amiya. 2011. 'Rethinking Comparative Literature', *Sahitya*: Journal of the Comparative Literature Association of India, no. 1: 9–18.

Devi, Mahasweta. 1997a. *Doulati*. New Delhi: R.K. Publishers.

———. 1997b. 'Gauhan', in *Doulati*. New Delhi: R.K. Publishers.

———. 1997c. 'Palamo', in *Doulati*. New Delhi: R.K. Publishers.

———. 1997d. *Breast Stories*. Trans. by Gayatri Chakravorty Spivak. Calcutta: Seagull Books.

———. 2001a. *Imaginary Maps*, 2nd edition. Trans. by Gayatri Chakravorty Spivak. Calcutta: Thema.

Devy, G.N. 2011. *A Nomad Called Thief: Reflections on Adivasi Silence*. New Delhi: Orient Blackswan Private Limited.

Dorson, Richard M. 1957. 'Identification of Folklore in American Literature', *Folklore in Literature: A Symposium*, in *The American Folklore*, 70 (275): 1–8. URL: http://www.jstor.org/stable/536498 (accessed on 26.06.2013).

Dundes, Alan. 1965. 'The Study of Folklore in Literature and Culture: Identification and Interpretation', *The Journal of American Folklore*, American Folklore Society, 78 (308): 136–142. URL: http://www.jstor.org/stable/538280 (accessed on 26.06.2013).

Durham, Meenakshi Gigi and Douglas M. Kellner (eds). 2006. *Media and Cultural Studies: Key Works*. Malden, Oxford and Victoria: Blackwell Publishing.

Dutta, Juri. 2012. *Ethnicity in the Fiction of Lummer Dai and Yeshe Dorjee Thongchi: A New Historicist Study*. New Delhi: Adhyayan Publishers and Distributors.

Dwivedi, A.N. 2004. 'Shashi Deshpande's *That Long Silence* (88): A Feminist Reading', in Mithilesh K. Pandey (ed.), *Writing the Female: Akademi Awarded Novels in English*. New Delhi: Sarup and Sons, pp. 139–148.

Edgar, Andrew and Peter Sedgwick. 2008. *Cultural Theory: The Key Concepts*. New York and London: Routledge.
Elwin, Verrier. 1958. *Myths of the North-East Frontier of India*. Itanagar: Directorate of Research, Government of Arunachal Pradesh.
———. 1959. *A Philosophy for NEFA*. Itanagar: Directorate of Research, Government of Arunachal Pradesh.
———. 1970. *A New Book of Tribal Fiction*. Itanagar: Directorate of Research, Government of Arunachal Pradesh.
Emecheta, Buchi. 1988. 'Feminism with a Small "f"', in Kirsten Holst Petersen (ed.), *Criticism and Ideology: Second African Writer's Conference*. Sweden: Scandinavian Institute of African Studies, pp. 173–185.
Fenton, Steve. 1999. *Ethnicity: Racism, Class and Culture*. Macmillan: London.
Fine, Michelle. 1998. 'Working the Hyphens: Reinventing Self and Other', in N.K. Denzin and Y.S. Lincoln (eds), *The Landscape of Qualitative Research*. Thousand Oaks: SAGE, pp. 130–155.
Fister, B. 1995. *Third World Women's Literature: A Dictionary and Guide to Materials in English*. London: Greenwood.
Friedman, Jonathan. 1999. 'Indigenous Struggles and the Discreet Charm of the Bourgeoisie', *Journal of World-Systems Research*, V (2): 391–411.
Furer-Haimendorf, C. von. 1977. 'The Changing Position of Tribal Populations in India', *RAIN*, 22: 2–8.
Gausset, Quentin, Justin Kenrick and Robert Gibb. 2011. 'Indigeneity and Autochthony: A Couple of False Twins?' *Social Anthropology*, 19 (2): 135–142.
George, K.M. (ed.). 1997. *Masterpieces of Indian Literature*. New Delhi: National Book Trust.
Goel, Savita. 1999. 'Tribal Women in the Selected Works of Mahasweta Devi', in Jaidipsingh K. Dodiya and K.V. Surendran (eds), *Indian Women Writers: Critical Perspectives*. New Delhi: Sarup and Sons, pp. 203–210.
Gohain, Hiren. 2002. *The New Millennium Pronouncing Anglo-Assamese Dictionary*. Guwahati: Banalata.
Goswami, Stuti. 2012. 'Terang's *Rongmilir Hahi*' Muse India, 37. URL: http://www.museindia.com/featurecontent.asp?issid=37&id=2642 (accessed on 24.01.2012).
Gruber, William E. 1987. '"Non-Aristotelian" Theater: Brecht's and Plato's Theories of Artistic Imitation', *Comparative Drama*, 21 (3): 199–213. URL: http://www.jstor.org/stable/41153286 (accessed on 01.07.2013).
Guberman, Ross Mitchell (ed.). 1996. *Julia Kristeva Interviews*. New York: Columbia University Press.
Guha, Amalendu. 2006. *Planter Raj to Swaraj: Freedom Struggle and Electoral Politics in Assam*. New Delhi: Tulika Books.
Guha, Sumit. 1999. *Environment and Ethnicity in India, 1200-1991*. Cambridge: Cambridge University Press.

Gunew, Sneja. 1994. *Framing Marginality: Multicultural Literary Studies*. Melbourne: Melbourne University Press.
Guttman, Anna. 2007. *The Nation of India in Contemporary Indian Literature*. New York: Palgrave Macmillan.
Haffman, Daniel G. 1957. 'Folklore in Literature: Notes toward a Theory of Interpretation', *Folklore in Literature: A Symposium*, in *The American Folklore*, 70 (275): 15–24. URL: http://www.jstor.org/stable/536498 (accessed on 26.06.2013).
Haffman, Daniel G., Richard M. Dorson, Carvel Collins and John W. Ashton. 1957. 'Folklore in Literature: A Symposium', *The Journal of American Folklore*, American Folklore Society, 70 (275): 1–24. URL: http://www.jstor.org/stable/536498 (accessed on 26.06.2013).
Hall, Stuart. 1997. *Representation: Cultural Representations and Signifying Practices*. London: SAGE.
Halliwell, Stephen. 1990. 'Aristotelian Mimesis Reevaluated', *Journal of the History of Philosophy*, 28 (4): 487–510.
Hannam, J. 2007. *Feminism*. Edinburgh: Pearson Education Limited.
Hogan, Patrick Colm, and Lalita Pandit. 1995. *Literary India: Comparative Studies in Aesthetics, Colonialism and Culture*. Albany: State University of New York Press.
Hogan, Patrick Colm. 1997. 'Literary Universals', *Poetics Today*, 18 (2): 223–249. URL: http://www.jstor.org/stable/1773433 (accessed on 06.01.2012).
Hutchinson, John and Anthony D. Smith (eds). 1996. *Ethnicity*. Oxford: Oxford University Press.
———. 1996. 'Introduction', in J. Hutchinson and A.D. Smith (eds), *Ethnicity*. Oxford and New York: Oxford University Press, pp. 1–14.
Indra, C. T. and Meenakshi Shivram (eds). 1999. *Post-Coloniality: Reading Literature*. New Delhi: Vikas Publishing House.
Jain, Jasbir and Avadhesh Kumar Singh (eds). 2001. *Indian Feminisms*. New Delhi: Creative Books.
Johnson-odim Cheryl. 1991. 'Common Themes, Different Contexts: Third World Women and Feminism', in Chandra Talpade Mohanty, Ann Russo and Lourdes Torres (eds), *Third World Women and the Politics of Feminism*. Bloomington and Indianapolis: Indiana University Press, pp. 314–327.
Jones, Sian. 1997. *The Archaeology of Ethnicity: Constructing Identities in the Past and Present*. London and New York: Routledge.
Jost, Francois. 1974. *Introduction to Comparative Literature*. New York: Bobbs-Merrill.
Karlsson, Bengt G. 2003. 'Anthropology and the "Indigenous Slot": Claims to and Debates about Indigenous Peoples' Status in India', *Critique of Anthropology*, 23 (4): 403–423.
Kristeva, Julia. 2001. 'Woman Can Never be Defined', in Mary Eagleton (ed.), *Feminist Literary Theory: A Reader*. West Sussex: Wiley-Blackwell, pp. 261–262.

Krupat, Arnold. 1992. *Ethnocriticism: Ethnography, History, Literature*. Berkeley: University of California.
Kurane, Anjali. 1999. *Ethnic Identity and Social Mobility*. Jaipur: Rawat Publications.
Lentricchia, Frank and Thomas McLaughlin (eds). 1995. *Critical Terms for Literary Study*. Chicago: University of Chicago Press.
Lewis, Mary Ellen B. 1976. 'Beyond Content in the Analysis of Folklore in Literature: Chinua Achebe's *Arrows of God*', *Research in African Literature*, Indiana University Press, 7 (1): 44–52. URL: http://www.jstor.org/stable/3819009 (accessed on 26.06.2013).
Lindfors, Berth O. 1972. 'Oral Tradition and the Individual Literary Talent', *Studies in the Novel*, Commonwealth Novel, University of New Texas, 4 (2): 200–217. URL: http://www.jstor.org/stable/29531515 (accessed on 26.06.2013).
Majumdar, D.N. and T.N. Madan. 1988. *An Introduction to Social Anthropology*. New Delhi: National Publishing House.
Majumdar, Swapan. 2011. 'Comparative Literature: Indian Dimensions', *Sahitya*: Journal of the Comparative Literature Association of India, no. 1: 31–38.
McArthur, Herbert. 1961. 'In Search of the Indian Novel', *The Massachusetts Review*, 2 (4): 600–613. URL: http://www.jstor.org/stable/25086722 (accessed on 22.05.2013).
McKeon, Richard. 1936. 'Literary Criticism and the Concept of Imitation in Antiquity', *Modern Philology*, 34 (1): 1–35.
Miner, Earl. 1990. *Comparative Poetics: An Intercultural Essay on Theories of Literature*. Princeton: Princeton University Press.
Misra, Tilottama. 1997. 'Crossing Linguistic Boundaries: Two Arunachali Writers in Search of Readers', *Economic and Political Weekly*, 42 (36): 3653–3661.
———. 2001. 'The Multi-Cultural Dimensions of the Asamiya Novel', *Indian Horizons* (Guest editor: Mrinal Miri), 48 (3): 26–37. New Delhi: ICCR.
Mohanty, Chandra Talpade. 1991. 'Under Western Eyes: Feminist Scholarship and Colonial Discourses', in Chandra Talpade Mohanty, Ann Russo and Lourdes Torres (eds), *Third World Women and the Politics of Feminism*. Bloomington: Indiana University Press, pp. 51–80.
Mohanty, Prafulla Kumar. 2013. 'The Novels of Pratibha Ray', *The Odisha Review*, LXIX (6): 37–42.
Moi, Toril. 1988. *Sexual/Textual Politics: Feminist Literary Theory*. New York: Methuen.
Morgan, Lewis Henry. 1982. *Ancient Society*. Calcutta: K.P. Bagghi & Co.
Morton, Stephen. 2003. *Gayatri Chakravorty Spivak*. New York: Routledge.
Moss, Jessica. 2007. 'What Is Imitative Poetry and Why Is It Bad?' in G.R.F. Ferrari (ed.), *The Cambridge Companion to Plato's Republic*. Cambridge: Cambridge University Press, pp. 415–444.
Mukherjee, Meenakshi. 1984. 'Reality and Realism: Indian Women as Protagonists in Four Nineteenth Century Novels', *Economic and Political Weekly*, 19 (2): 76–85. URL: http://www.jstor.org/stable/4372842 (accessed on 07.01.2010).

Mukherjee, Meenakshi. 2001. *The Twice Born Fiction*. New Delhi: Oxford University Press.
———. 2008. *Elusive Terrain: Culture and Literary Memory*. New Delhi: Oxford University Press.
Murdock, G. 1999. 'Corporate Dynamics and Broadcasting Futures', in H. Mackay and T. O'Sullivan (eds), *The Media Reader: Continuity and Transformation*. London: SAGE, pp. 28–42.
Nanda, Meera. 1996. 'The Science Question in Post-Colonial Feminism', *Economic and Political Weekly*, 31 (16/17): WS2–WS8.
Narayan, Kirin. 1993. 'How Native is a "Native" Anthropologist?' *American Anthropologist*, 95 (3): 671–686. URL: http://www.jstor.org/stable/679656 (accessed on 28.09.2011).
———. 1999. 'Ethnography and Fiction: Where is the Border?' *Anthropology and Humanism*, 24 (2): 134–147. URL: http://onlinelibrary.wiley.com/doi/10.1525/ahu.1999.24.2.134/pdf (accessed on 22.09.2011).
Narayan. 2011. *Kocharethi*. Trans. by Catherine Thankamma. New Delhi: Oxford University Press.
Natarajan, Nalini. 1996. *Handbook of Twentieth-Century Literatures of India*. United States of America: Greenwood Publishing.
Nath, Debarshi P. and Juri Dutta. 2012. 'Africa and India in the Novels of Dai and Emecheta', *Comparative Literature and Culture*, 14 (2): 1–10.
Neog, Dimbeswar. 1962. *New Lights on the History of Asamiya Literature*. Guwahati: Suwani Prakash.
Neog, Maheshwar. 1985. *Early History of the Vaisnava Faith and Movement in Assam: Sankaradev and his Times*, 2nd edition (reprint). New Delhi: Motilal Banarsidass.
Niezen, Ronald. 2003. *The Origins of Indigenism: Human Rights and the Politics of Identity*. Berkeley: University of California Press.
Orman, Stanley. 1970. 'The Resignation: A Fully Indian Novel', *Mahfil*, 6 (4): 61–72. URL: http://www.jstor.org/stable/40874392 (accessed on 22.05.2013).
Paci, F.G. 1985. 'Tasks of the Canadian Novelist Writing on Immigrant Themes', in J. Pivato (ed.), *Contrasts: Comparative Essays on Italian-Canadian Writing*. Montreal: Guernica Editions.
Pandey, Mithilesh K. (ed.). 2004. *Writing the Female: Akademi Awarded Novels in English*. New Delhi: Sarup and Sons.
Panja, Shormishtha (ed.). 2001. *Many Indias, Many Literatures: New Critical Essays*. Delhi: Worldview Publications.
Pappas, Nickolas. 1995. *Plato and the Republic*. London: Routledge.
Pathy, Jaganath. 1992. 'Tribal and Indigenous Peoples of the World', in B. Chaudhury (ed.), *Tribal Transformation in India, Vol. 3: Ethnopolitics and Identity*. New Delhi: Inter India Publication, pp. 13–27.
Pivato, Joseph. 1996. 'Representation of Ethnicity as Problem: Essence or Construction', *Journal of Canadian Studies*, Peterborough, Fall 31 (3): 48.

Plain, Gill and Susan Sellers. 2007. 'Introduction', in Gill Plain and Susan Sellers (eds), *A History of Feminist Literary Criticism*. Cambridge: Cambridge University Press.
Pushpa, Maitreyi. 2006. *Alma Kabutari*. Trans. by Raji Narasimhan. New Delhi: Katha.
Rathod, Jaswant. 2013. 'Positioning the Subaltern in Post-Colonial India: A Socio-Cultural and Environmental Study of Mahasweta Devi's "Pterodactyl"', *Research Scholar* 1 (2): 49–56.
Ray, Pratibha. 2001. *The Primal Land*. Trans. by Bikram K. Das. New Delhi: Orient Longman Limited.
Reed, Pamela Yaa Asanteewa. 2001. 'Africana Womanism and African Feminism: A Philosophical, Literary and Cosmological Dialectic on Family', *The Western Journal of Black Studies*, 25 (3): 168–176.
Remak, Henry H.H. 1961. 'Comparative Literature: Its Definition and Function', in Newton P. Stallknecht and Horst Frenz (eds), *Comparative Literature: Method and Perspective*. Carbondale: Southern Illinois University Press.
Robinson, Mairi (ed.). 1997. *The Chambers 21st Century Dictionary*. New Delhi: Allied Chambers (India) Limited.
Roy Burman, B.K. 1992. 'Transformation of Tribes and Analogous Social Formations', in B. Chaudhury (ed.), *Tribal Transformation in India, Vol. 3: Ethnopolitics and Identity*. New Delhi: Inter India Publication, pp. 28–34.
Roy, Arundhati. 2011. *Broken Republic*. Delhi: Penguin.
Ruthven, K.K. 1990. *Feminist Literary Studies: An Introduction*. Melbourne: Cambridge University Press.
Ryan, Michael. 2002. *Literary Theory: A Practical Introduction*, 2nd edition. Oxford: Blackwell Publications.
Sangari, Kumkum and Sudesh Vaid (eds). 2006. *Recasting Women: Essays in Colonial History*. New Delhi: Zubaan.
Saraswati, B. (ed.). 1991. *Tribal Thought and Culture*. New Delhi: Concept Publishing Company.
Sarma, G.P. 2010. 'Tribal Tradition in Assamese Novel', Trans. by Radhika Barua, *Muse India*, 31. URL: http://www.museindia.com/viewarticle.asp?myr=2010&issid=31&id=1955 (accessed on 08.09.2011).
Selden, Raman, Peter Widdowson and Peter Brooker. 2005. *A Reader's Guide to Contemporary Literary Theory*. Harlow: Pearson Education Limited.
Sellers, Susan. 2001. *Myth and Fairy Tale in Contemporary Women's Fiction*. London: Palgrave.
Sen, Nivedita and Nikhil Yadav (eds). 2008. *Mahasweta Devi: An Anthology of Recent Criticism*. New Delhi: Pencraft International.
Shahani, Roshan G. and Shoba V. Ghosh. 2000. 'Indian Feminist Criticism: In Search of New Paradigms Source', *Economic and Political Weekly*, 35 (43/44): 3813–3816.

Sharma, Jayeeta. 2012. *Empire's Garden: Assam and the Making of India*. Ranikhet: Permanent Black.

Shiva, Vandana.1988. *Staying Alive: Women, Ecology and Survival in India*. New Delhi: Kali for Women.

———.1991. *Ecology and the Politics of Survival: Conflicts over Natural Resources in India*. New Delhi: SAGE.

Showalter, Elaine. 1977. *A Literature of Their Own*. Princeton: Princeton University Press.

———. 1979 [2012]. *Towards a Feminist Poetics*. USA and Canada: Routledge.

Simon, Sherry. 1996. *Gender in Translation: Cultural Identity and the Politics of Transmission*. London and New York: Routledge.

Singh, Satendra R. 1989. 'Towards a Concept of an Indian Novel: A Thematic Construct', in Amiya Dev and Sisir Kumar Das (eds), *Comparative Literature: Theory and Practice*. Simla: Indian Institute of Advanced Study.

Smith, Anthony D. 1998. *Nationalism and Modernism*. London: Routledge.

Sollors, Werner. 1995. 'Ethnicity', in *Critical Terms for Literary Study*. Chicago: University of Chicago Press.

Spender, Dale. 1980. *Man Made Language*. London: Routledge.

Srikanth, H. and C.J. Thomas. 2005. 'Naga Resistance Movement and the Peace Process in Northeast India', *Peace and Democracy in South Asia*, 1 (2): 57–87.

Tamuli, Girin and R.N. Koley. 2006. 'Yeshe Dorjee Thongchi', *Silifor Review*, 2 (II): 41–48.

Tharu, Susie and K. Lalitha. 1993. *Women Writing in India*. New York: Feminist Press.

Thiong'o, Ngugi wa. 1987. *Decolonising the Mind: The Politics of Language in African Literature*. Harare: Zimbabwe Publishing House. URL: http://www.jstor.org/stable/4405387 (accessed on 28.06.2010).

Thongchi, Yeshe Dorjee. 2005. *Sonam*. Trans. by Mridula Borooah. Guwahati: Spectrum Publications.

———. 2010. *Silent Lips Murmuring Hearts*. Trans. by Debarshi Prasad Nath. New Delhi: Sahitya Akademi.

Vashista, Anita. 2006. 'Redefining Feminine Space and Aesthetics: A Study of Maitreyi Pushpa's *Edennmam* and *Chaak*', *Muse India*, 7. URL: http://www.museindia.com/viewarticle.asp?myr=2006&issid=7&id=293 (accessed on 27.01.2012).

Wellek, Rene and Austin Warren. 1949. *Theory of Literature*. New York: Harcourt, Brace and Company.

Wenzel, Jennifer. 1998. 'Epic Struggles over India's Forest in Mahasweta Devi's Short Fiction', *Journal of Comparative Poetics*, no. 18: 127–158. URL: http://www.jstor.org/stable/521884 (accessed on 28.06.2010).

Wiener, Myron. 1978. *Sons of the Soil: Migration and Ethnic Conflict in India*. New Delhi: Oxford University Press.

Wolf, E.R. 1994. 'Perilous Ideas: Race, Culture, People', *Current Anthropology,* 35 (1): 1–12.
Wolfe Thomas. 1943. *Look Homeward Angel.* New York: Charles Scribner's Sons.
Xaxa, Virginious. 2003. 'Tribes in India', in Veena Das (ed.), *Oxford India Companion to Sociology and Social Anthropology.* New Delhi: Oxford University Press, pp. 373–404.
Yinger, J. Milton. 1997. *Ethnicity: Source of Strength? Source of Conflict?* Jaipur: Rawat Publications.
Zepetnek, Steven Tötösy de. 1998. *Comparative Literature: Theory, Method, Application.* Amsterdam: Rodopi.
––––––– (ed.). 2005. *Comparative Cultural Studies and Michael Ondaatje's Writing.* West Lafayette: Purdue University Press.

Assamese

Baruah, Amulya. 1973.*Ukhun Jangha* (My Treasure). Guwahati: Guwahati Book Stall.
Baruah, Bikashjyoti. 2006. *Pahari Kanya* (Daughter of the Hills). Guwahati: Jyoti Prakashan.
Barua, Navakanta. 1953. *Kapilipariya Xadhu* (The Story by the Side of the Kapili River). Guwahati: Lawyers Book Stall.
Barua, Rasna. 1997. *Seuji Patar Kahini* (The Story of the Green Leaves, 2nd edition). Nalbari: Journal Emporium.
Bharadwaj, Pashupati. 1965. *Simsangar Dutipar* (The Two Sides of the Simsang River). Calcutta: Asom Book Depot.
Bhattacharjee, Birendrakumar. 2003. *Iyaruingom,* 7th edition. Guwahati: Lawyers Book Stall.
Bora, Dilip. 2000. 'Exa Bacharar Axamiya Upanyaxot Janajatiya Jibonor Chitra' (The Picture of Tribal Life as Reflected in the Assamese Novels of Hundred Years), in Nagen Thakur (ed.), *Exa Bacharar Axamiya Upanyax* (Assamese Novels of One Hundred Years). Guwahati: Jyoti Prakashan, pp. 122–141.
Bora, Sarna. 1986. *Diyung Nadir Geet* (The Song of the Diyung River). Guwahati: Lawyers Book Stall.
–––––––. 1987. *Simsang Nadir Hanhi* (The Smile of the Simsang River). Nagaon: Sushil Prakash.
Bordoloi, Rajanikanta. 2007. *Miri Jiyori* (The Mising Damsel) in B.K. Sharma (ed.), *Rajanikanta Bordoloir Upanyas Samagra.* Guwahati: Sarada Publication.
Borpujari, Jitanjali. 1999. *Asomiya Upanyasat Janajatiya Jivan* (Tribal Life in Assamese Novel). Guwahati: Chandra Prakash.
–––––––. 2000. 'Exa Bacharar Asamiya Upanyaxor Samridhit Janajatiyo Lekhokor Abodan' (The Contribution of Tribal Writers in the Development of the

Assamese Novels of Hundred Years), in Nagen Thakur (ed.), *Exa Bacharar Axamiya Upanyax* (Assamese Novels of One Hundred Years). Guwahati: Jyoti Prakashan, pp. 109–121.

Dai, Lummer. 1961. *Paharar Xile Xile* (In the Midst of the Hills). Guwahati: Asom Prakashan Parishad.

———. 1963. *Prithivir Hanhi* (Laughter of the Earth). Guwahati: Asom Prakashan Parishad.

———. 1967. *Mon aru Mon* (Different Minds). Guwahati: Dutta Baruah and Co.

———. 2003. *Upar Mahal* (Higher Levels). Guwahati: Bani Mandir.

———. 2004. *Kanyar Mulya* (Bride Price, 2nd edition). Guwahati: Bani Mandir.

Das, Jogesh. 1955. *Dawar Aru Nai* (Clouds Have Gone). Guwahati: Lawyers Book Stall.

Devi, Mahasweta. 1995. *Mahasweta Devir Swanirbasita Galpa* (Self-Selected Stories of Mahasweta Devi). Trans. by Tilak Hazarika. New Delhi: National Book Trust.

———. 2001b. *Aranyer Adhikar* (Rights of the Forest, 2nd edition). Trans. by Kulanath Gogoi. New Delhi: Sahitya Akademi.

Dutta Goswami, Prafulla. 1952. *Kecha Patar Kapani* (The Tremor of the Green Leaves). Guwahati: Bina Library.

Kalita, Arupa Patangia. 2003. *Felani*. Guwahati: Jyoti Prakashan.

Mipun, Jatin. 1993. *Miksijili* (Stream of Teardrops). Guwahati: Students' Stores.

Neog, Maheswar. 2010. *Asomiya Sahityar Ruprekha* (An Outline of the Assamese Literature, 2nd edition). Guwahati: Chandra Prakash.

Pegu, Sishuram. 2006. *Dhansiri Ganwar Dekajan* (The Young Man from the Dhansiri Village). Bokakhat: Puoti Sahitya Sabha.

Phukan, Jadav. 1982. *Mekroki*. Diphu: Bho-Mongbhi-Achong.

———. 1989. *Kengwat Kasedong* (Walking on One's Footprints, 2nd edition). Diphu: The Author.

Rabha, Bishnu. 1989. *Mising Koneng* (Mising Girl), in Jogesh Das and Sarbeswar Bora (eds), *Bishnurabha Rachanawali: I*, pp. 643–680.

Rongpi, Jayanta. 1977. *Puwate Ejak Dhanesh* (A Flight of Hornbills at Dawn). Karbi Anglong: Karbi Youth Farming Society, Dokmoka.

Pam, Rajen. 1990. *Janong Jinong* (Live Life). Guwahati: Lawyers Book Stall.

Pamegam, Tarun Chandra. 1989. *Xamajar Xesh Ximat* (At the Final Border of Society), in Bhrigumoni Kagyung (ed.), *Tarun Chandra Pamegam Rachanawali: I*.

Pegu, Bhaben. 1987. *Oiaow* (Beautiful). Guwahati: Ramani Das.

Sarma, Hemanta Kumar. 1972. *Asamiya Sahityat Dristipat* (A Look at the Assamese Literature). New Book Stall: Guwahati.

Sarma, Kailash. 1963. *Anami Nagini* (The Nameless Naga Girl). Calcutta: Progressive Publishers.

———. 1971. *Dalimir Xapon* (The Dreams of Dalimi). Guwahati: Bani Prakash.

———. 1990. *Bidrohi Nagar Hatat* (In the Hands of the Rebel Nagas, 3rd edition). Guwahati: Banalata.

Sarma, Satyendranath. 1965. *Asamiya Sahityar Itibritta* (An Account of the Assamese Literature). Bani Prakash, Pathsala.
———. 1976. *Asomiya Upanyasar Gatidhara* (The Current of the Assamese Novel). Guwahati: Bani Mandir.
———. 2009. *Asomiya Sahityar Samikhyatmak Itibritta* (An Account of the Assamese Literature of the Past). Guwahati: Soumar Prakash.
Sarma, Umakanta. 1986. *Ejak Manuh Ekhan Aranya* (A Herd of People, A Forest). Guwahati: Lawyers Book Stall.
———. 1992. *Bharand Pakhir Jak* (A Flock of Vulture-type Birds). Guwahati: Lawyers Book Stall.
Terang, Rong Bong. 1993. *Rongmilir Hanhi* (The Laughter of Rongmili). Guwahati: Asom Prakashan Parishad.
Thakur, Nagen (ed.). 2000. *Exa Bacharar Axamiya Upanyax* (Assamese Novels of One Hundred Years). Jyoti Prakashan: Guwahati.
Thongchi, Yeshe Dorjee. 1981. *Sonam*. Nalbari: Journal Emporium.
———. 1983. *Lingjhik* (A Pillar). Guwahati: Dutta Baruah and Co.
———. 2001. *Mouno Ounth Mukhar Hriday* (Silent Lips Murmuring Hearts). Guwahati: Banalata.
———. 2004. *Sava Kota Manuh* (The Man Who Slices Dead Bodies). Guwahati: Banalata.
———. 2005. *Sonam*. Guwahati: Parbati Prakashan.

Hindi

Gupta, Ramanika (ed.). 2002. *Adivasi Swar Aur Nayi Shatabdi* (Adivasi Voice and New Century). New Delhi: Vani Prakashan.

Magazines, Newspapers, Interviews (English and Assamese)

Dutta, Ajanta. 2002. 'Lummer Dair Sandhanat' (In Search of Lummer Dai), in Ajit Kumar Bhuyan (ed.), *Aaji*. Guwahati, 3 February.
Shiva, Vandana. 2007. *Development Cooperation Handbook*/Interviews/ Vandana Shiva. Wilma Massucco. Rishikesh. URL: http://en.wikibooks.org/wiki/Development_Cooperation_Handbook/Interviews/Vandana_Shiva
Thongchi, Yeshe Dorjee. 2006. 'Mor Sahitya Sarchar Bisoye Mor Baktabya' (My Views Regarding My Writings), in Homen Borgohain (ed.), *Satsori*. Guwahati. 1–15 March.

Index

Achebe, Chinua, 94
Adibhumi, 77–79, 85
adivasis tribe/society, 35, 53, 67–68, 83, 86–87, 96, 103
Agarwalla, Chandrakumar, 38
Agarwalla, Jyoti Prasad, 38
Ahmad, Aijaz, 22, 24
Ahom tribe, 33n1
All Assam Gana Sangram Parishad (AAGP), 34n2
All Assam Students Union (AASU), 34n2
Alyokeshi Beshyar Bishay (The Case of Alokeshi, the Prostitute), 37–38
American white feminist criticism, 129
Anami Nagini, 45
Anderson, Benedict, 74
Anthropological Survey of India, 5
anthropologists, 3–7
 native and non-native, 39
appropriation of voice, 2
Aranyer Adhikar (Mahasweta Devi), 83–85
Aristotle, 13, 15
Arunachal Pradesh, 74
Asamiya, 35
Asom Gana Parishad, 34n2
Asom Sahitya Sabha, 116
Assam
 British introduced Bengali as court language of, 33
 category of 'the Assamese', 35
Assam agitation (1979–1985), 34
Assamese ethnic novels, 40
Assamese literature, 36–62

Assamese novels, 2
Assam (Official) Language Act (ALA), 36

Barth, Fredrik, 10
Barua, Hem, 38
Barua, Navakanta, 38
Baviskar, Amita, 83
bayen (witch), 121–122
Bennett, Paul A., 91
Bernheimer, Charles, 41
Beteille, Andre, 4, 11
Bezbaroa, Lakshminath, 38
Bhattacharjya, Birendra Kumar, 38, 45
Bijuli (Lightning), 42
Bimala Prasad Chaliha government, 36
Bonda tribe/community, 78–80, 82, 85
 negligence by British, 88
 salap tree value for, 88
Borang, Kaling, 50
Bordoloi, Rajanikanta, 43
Borpujari, Jitanjali, 105
Bortika, 83
Buddhism, 101–102
Burman, B.K. Roy, 3–4
Butler, Judith, 112

caste, 5. *See also* tribes
Chhotanagpur area tribes, 85
Christianity, 106–108
Clifford, James, 40–41
Cohen, Ronald, 10
colonial masters, 62, 88
colonial nation states, 11
comparative cultural studies, concept of, 32

comparative literature, 23, 25–30
  approaches in, 30–32
Comparative Literature in the Age of Multiculturalism (Charles Bernheimer), 29
Cowen, Michael, 70
cultural groups, 8
cultural insiders, 40
  problematizing identity of author, 62–68
cultural outsiders, 40, 42, 62–63, 68
cultural turn, 39

Dai, Lummer, 36, 50–51, 53, 61, 98, 109
Dalimir Sopon (Kailash Sarma), 45
Derrida, Jacques, 132
Dev, Amiya, 26–27
developing countries women, 113–114
development, 70, 72
  ceaseless process, 71
Devy, G.N., 71, 73, 81
Dikus, 85–86
divergence, 131
Dorson, Richard M., 92
Durham, Meenakshi Gigi, 18–19
Dwivedi, A.N., 114

Ecology and the Politics of Survival: Conflicts over Natural Resources in India, 71
empathic universals, 31
The Empire Writes Back (Patrick Hogan), 31
Environment and Ethnicity in India (Sumit Guha), 128
ethnic Assamese community, 35
ethnic communities of India, 30
ethnic group formation, 89
ethnic groups, 7–13
ethnic homelands, claims for, 130
ethnicity, 7–10, 61, 89. *See also* tribes
  in Indian novels, 2
ethnic mobilization, 110

ethnic nationalism, 129–130
ethnic novels, concept of, 30, 39
ethnic novels in Assamese, 32
ethnic societies, 9
ethnocriticism, 73
ethnographic account, 41
ethnographic fiction, 41
ethnographic novels, 43, 49, 67, 90, 94
ethnographic writings, 40–41
ethnography, 40, 131
Eurocentrism, 32

Fawcett, Milicent, 111
feminism, concept of, 111–114, 118
feminism interrogates patriarchal structure of society, 129
feminists, 16, 18, 111
  consciousness, 121
  critique, 116
  literary criticism, 112
  literature, 115
  movements, 113
  phase, 116
  space, 119
  writers, 112
Ferenggadaw (Medini Choudhury), 48
fiction, 102, 131
folk beliefs, 91–93, 95, 98–99
folk customs, 93, 95, 99
folklore
  elements of, 93
  in literature, 92
  offers understanding of creative writing, 92
  use of, 91
folkloric materials, 91
  significance in literary uses of, 93–94
folktales, 91
forest, 69–89
  culture, 71
Foucault, Michel, 132
Fried, Morton, 4
Furer-Haimendorf, Von, 108

Gandhi, Indira, 124
Goel, Savita, 120–121, 123
Goswami, Hemchandra, 38
Goswami, Indira, 38
Goswami, Stuti, 107
Guha, Amalendu, 34
gulang babu, 85
gynocritics, 116

Haffman, Daniel G., 93–94
Hazarika, Atul Chandra, 38
Hazarika, Bhupen, 36, 61
heterogeneity of Indian tribes, 1
historical romance, 39
Hogan, Patrick, 31
human rights, 69–89, 130

identity of indigenous ethnic groups, 12
identity politics of Assam, 33–36
imagined community, 74
imagined geography, 74
imesis, Aristotelian concept of, 15
imitation, 13
Indian literature, concept of, 20–24
Indian novel, concept of, 19–25
  division of, 39
indigeneity, concept of, 11–12
indigenous people/tribes, 11–12
  marginalization of, 89
Itum, Borgam, 118

Jatrikor Jatra, 37, 42
Jayasree, G.S., 97, 104
Jnanapith award, 84
Jonaki (Moonlight), 38

Kaminikanta, 37
Kandali, Madhav, 37
Kanyar Mulya, 53
Kapilipariya Sadhu (Navakanta Barua), 43
Karbi society, 56, 58, 106
Karbi writers contribution to Assamese literature, 57

Kecha Patar Kapani (Prafulla Dutta Goswami), 43, 48
Kellner, Douglas M., 18–19
Kengwat Kasedong (Jadav Phukan), 47
Kerala Sahitya Akademi award, 96
Khagen Pegu, 36
Khasi society, 47
Kipling, Rudyard, 88
Kocharethi (Kirin Narayan), 94, 96, 99, 103, 106–109
Kondh tribe, 79
Kristeva, Julia, 113
Krupat, Arnold, 40, 132

Lacan, Jacques, 132
likenesses, 15
Lingjhik (Yeshe Dorjee Thongchi), 54–55
linguistic identity of Assam, 33–36
linguistic nationalism, concept of, 33–34
Literary India: Comparative Studies in Aesthetics, Colonialism, and Culture, (Patrick Hogan and Lalita Pandit), 30
literary texts, 1–2, 12
literary universals, search for, 30–32
literature, 127
  use as folkloric materials, 91
A Literature of Their Own (Elaine Showalter), 116
literary reality, 15
Lukács, Georg, 15

Magsaysay award, 84
Mahabharata, 23, 37, 90, 121
mahajan, 106
Mahasweta Devi, 83–84, 86–87, 89, 111–130, 132
Mahayana Buddhists, 101
Majumdar, Swapan, 28
Malayarayar tribe/community, 96–98, 104, 109
Man Made Language (Dale Spender), 16

marginal community, 3
marginal group, 2
marginalized communities women, 113–114
Maybury-Lewis, David, 12
McArthur, Herbert, 23
McKeon, Richard, 13
Mekroki (Jadav Phukan), 47
Memorandum of Settlement (MoS) between Indian government and Assam movement leaders (1985), 35n3
middle-class Assamese people, 35
middle-class white women, 113
Mill, John Stuart, 115
Miner, Earl, 27
minority group, 2
Mipun, Jatin, 59
Miri Jiyori (The Mising Damsel), 42–43
Mising community/tribe, 42–43, 55–56, 59–60, 95–96
Mising Koneng (Bishnu Rabha), 55
Miss X or the Wolf Woman (Christine Crow), 110
Mitchell, W. J. T., 17
modern nation, 75
modern society, 106
modern Western feminist movement is, 112
Mohanty, Chandra Talpade, 129
Mohanty, Prafulla Kumar, 76
Mon aru Mon (Lummer Dai), 97–99, 103, 105
Monpa tribe/society, 54–55, 73, 95, 99, 101–102
Moorti Devi Award, 76
Morgan, Lewis Henry, 4
Mouno Ounth Mukhar Hriday (Yeshe Dorjee Thongchi), 54, 62–63, 71, 73–74
Mrityunjaya (Birendrakumar Bhattacharjee), 46
Mukherjee, Meenakshi, 21, 23–24, 28

multiethnic nature of Indian culture, 19–20
multiliterary nature of Indian culture, 19–20
Murdock, Graham, 18

Naga revolution, 45
Nagas tribe, 5
Nalini Bala Devi, 38
Nam Tair Haimu (Samsing Hanse), 57
Narayan, Kirin, 39–40, 90–110, 132
national identity, 75–76
nation-building process, 76
nation-orientation, 32
native anthropologists, 39
nature, exploitation of, 83
negotiate survival by Indian women, 114
Nehru–Elwinian policy towards North-East tribes, 70
Nehru, Jawaharlal, 69–70
Nehruvian path to nation-building, 70
non-Assamese novels, 2
non-Christian Karbis, 107
non-native anthropologists, 39
non-tribe, 6. *See also* tribes
North East ethnic groups, 11
North East Frontier Agency (NEFA), 55, 64, 69, 74, 76, 88. *See also* Arunachal Pradesh

Orissa Sahitya Akademi award, 76
Orman, Stanley, 23
Orunodoi (The Rise of the Sun), 37, 42

Pamegam, Tarun Chandra, 59
Pathy, Jaganath, 5–6
Pegu, Bhaben, 59
Pegu, Ganesh, 59
people speaking in same language, 4
The Piligrim's Progress (John Bunyan), 37
Plato, 13–15

Index 151

political realism, 39
postcolonialism, 104, 132
postcolonialists, 16
post-colonial nation states, 11
poststructuralism, 62
poststructuralists, 16, 90
Prahlada Charita (Hem Saraswati), 37
pre-Vaishnavite period of Assam, 37
psychological novels, 39
Pula, 99
Pushpa, Maitreyi, 127
Puwate Ejak Dhanesh (Jayanta Rongpi), 57

Rabha, Bishnu, 36, 61
Rabha society, 58
Rajan, Rajeshwari Sunder, 120
Ramayana (Valmiki), 37, 90
Rashtriya Swayamsevak Sangh (RSS), 108
Ray, Pratibha, 76, 81, 83, 88–89
realistic representation, 15
real reality, 15
Remak, Henry, 26
remo, 81
representation, concept of, 2, 13–19
Representation: Cultural Representations and Signifying Practices (Stuart Hall), 16
Rig Veda, 71
Rong Bong Terang, 36
Rongmilir Hanhi (Rong Bong Terang), 105–106, 108
Roy, Arundhati, 79
Ryan, Michael, 117

Sahlins tribe, 6
Sahu, Sitanath, 80
Said, Edward, 18
Saikia, Dilip, 64–66, 73, 75–76
Sangge, Aane, 100, 103
Santhals tribe, 5
Sarala Award, 76

sarbasa (village-headman), 105–106
Sarma, G.P., 106
Sava Kota Manuh (Yeshe Dorjee Thongchi), 29, 54, 99–102
second wave feminists, 112–113
Seuji Patar Kahini (Birinchi Kumar Baruah), 44, 62–63, 66–67, 78
Shan tribe, 33n1
Shenton, Robert, 70
Sherdukpen tribe/community, 54, 66, 73, 102
Shiva, Vandana, 72
Simantar Sur (Dhrubajyoti Bora), 47
Simsangar Dutipar (Pashupati Bharadwaj), 46
Simsang Nadir Hanhi (Sarna Bora), 48
Singh, Satendra R., 20, 28
Sitanath Brahma Choudhury award, 116
social realism, 39
Sonam (Yeshe Dorjee Thongchi), 54
Spivak, Gayatri Chakravorty, 121, 133
Staying Alive: Women, Ecology and Survival in India (Vandana Shiva), 72
structuralists, 16
subaltern forces to speak, danger of, 133
Sulung, 98

techniques, 31
Terang, Rong Bong, 36, 56, 90–110
That Long Silence (Shashi Deshpande), 114
Things Fall Apart (Chinua Achebe), 94
third wave feminists, 112–113
Third World countries, 111, 129
Third World feminisms, 129
Third World Movements, 72
Third World women, 133
Third World Women's Literature (Barbara Fister), 111
Thongchi, Yeshe Dorjee, 50–51, 54, 66, 73, 76, 88–89, 100, 109

traditional customs, 93
transgression of disciplinary boundaries, 132
Tribals in Indian English Novel (A.K. Chaturvedi), 49
tribes/tribal people, 1, 10. *See also* caste; ethnic groups
   British writing on Indian society, 5
   characteristics of, 7
   definition of, 3–6
   exploitation of, 83
   facing stiff competition from new trends in anthropology, 11
   idea as separate humanity, 7
   phases of, 5
   units of organization, 7

Ukhun Jangha (Amulya Barua), 46
Ulgulan movement, 86
United Nations, 12
Upar Mahal, 53–54, 61

Vashista, Anita, 127
Vidyasagar, Iswar Chandra, 115
Vishwa Hindu Parishad (VHP), 108

Warren, Austin, 25–26, 31
Wellek, René, 25–26, 31
Western colonialism, 104
Western feminism, 114
Wolf, Eric, 10
Wolfe, Thomas, 90–91
womanism, 114
women in ethnic communities, 115
writing fiction, 95

Xamajar Xesh Ximat (Tarun Chandra Pamegam), 59

Yandaboo Treaty of 1826, 33, 42
Yinger, J. Milton, 7

Zepetnek, Steven Tötösy de, 25–26, 32

About the Author

Juri Dutta is presently working as a Research Associate in the Centre for Assamese Studies, Tezpur University, Assam. She was awarded PhD from Rajiv Gandhi University, Arunachal Pradesh in 2007. She has published articles, poems, short stories in English and Assamese in several leading magazines and newspapers of Assam. A collection of her short stories (in Assamese) was published in 2009. Her book titled *Ethnicity in the Fiction of Lummer Dai and Yeshe Dorjee Thongchi: A New Historicist Approach* was published in 2012. She is presently carrying out research activities in the area of Assamese fiction. Her areas of interest include creative writing, regional fictions of India, ethnic literature, comparative literature and translation studies.